# PADDY DOHERTY
# IN MY OWN WORDS

First published electronically with Amazon 2021

ISBN 978 1 7399397 2 4

# CONTENTS

*Doherty is an Irish name from the Gaelic O'Dochartaigh, meaning 'descendant of Dochartach', whose name meant Obstructive, Unlucky or Hurtful.*

*The family were chieftains in Donegal.*

## _Well, Hello There..._

My name is Paddy Doherty. If you didn't know already, I am a Traveller of Irish descent. I was known for the TV programmes: _My Big Fat Gypsy Wedding and Danny Dyer's Deadliest Men_ and apparently this made me 'a celebrity'. When I was approached to take part in _Celebrity Big Brother_ in 2011, I was a bit wary about it, even my Daddy and my Roseanne said, "Don't do it, Paddy!"

But you know what? We Travellers and gypsies alike have a bad reputation. I wanted people to see the real Paddy Doherty, the son, the brother, the husband, the father, the grandfather and the true friend that I am. Really, truly and deeply inside me and maybe just… I don't know… see a different side to me that proved the reputation wrong. Just know this though… I have a large and extended family who mean the world to me; everything I do is to provide for them and protect them.

Like most people, I have had ups and downs in my life and none more so since winning _Celebrity Big Brother_ in 2011.

You have to know a little more about the way I live, what's important to me, how I think and feel about things, what's happened to me in the past and how that drives me forward and influences the way I am now.

I have been lucky, unlucky, blessed and cursed in my life since *Celebrity Big Brother*. I have met lots of people from all walks of life, I have travelled to far-off places I could never have dreamed of, I have done more TV programmes and appearances and I have experienced both joy and despair throughout that time. But you know what? I wouldn't be who I am today without those experiences.

At that crazy time, at the height of my 'celebrity' I felt like I was built up on a pedestal as high as a skyscraper: it was a dream, an absolutely beautiful dream, a dream so out of this world I never wanted to wake up.

I don't regard myself as a celebrity – you are what you are in life. Before I became famous on TV, I already had a great name in the travelling communities of the English, the Irish, the Scots and the Welsh. All over the country, they knew the name of Paddy Doherty, mostly in those days as the 'dealer man' I'd say. I'd swap and sell cars and do great deals. I'd even swap a car for a pair of shoes if the price was right! I was happy and I just loved life so much; I loved dealing and I loved people, and above all I had a great name. My God was good to me and I think He still is.

When I did deals in those days, men would come to me and say, "I'm sorry, Paddy, but I don't have the money yet," so I would give them the car on their word. Your word is everything in my community and I had the ability to read these men and just know instinctively if they were telling the truth. Many of my deals were done this way, on trust. I would say, "Listen, you give me the money when you have it, son. Come back in twelve months," and that was the deal done. I invented the '*Buy Now Pay Later*' offer! They would always come back and not one person ever missed, fiddled or ripped me off – it was an honest deal, done on a handshake, on trust and they would always pay me back in the end.

Every word of this is the truth about my life. These are my own words, reflections of what has influenced me, made me who I am, giving you that insight too and sharing what I've been doing or what has happened to me and my family and friends in the last ten years up to now; no hiding, no lies, no flowering things up, just the whole truth. It's good and it's sad – just like life is!

It's no secret that I'm dyslexic, poorly educated and still learning to read and write. I am not the greatest reader to this day, I can read a bit but it's very bad, that's dyslexia for you. These days thank God, they seem to pick up on dyslexia quickly, if that had happened for me when I was younger, I am sure I would have been able to learn how to read properly and spell but life is what it is sometimes.

So, know that this book is not polished and shined, but it is from my heart, in my words. Join me on my gambol through the verdant fields of my mind (I make no apology for the here, there and everywhere style of my book) – it's just the way my brian (oops, sorry, that would be BRAIN) works and the rollercoaster of my life. I hope you enjoy it and maybe learn a few things along the way!

## Celebrity Big Brother

I didn't really realise quite how high up I was in 'celebrity' terms after *My Big Fat Gypsy Wedding and Danny Dyer's Deadliest Men*, but like I said, apparently it made me 'a celebrity' and then out of the blue I was asked to do *Celebrity Big Brother*. I talked to my Daddy about it first, as I wasn't sure whether to do it or not.

"Old man, what do you reckon about this *Celebrity Big Brother* idea and me going in for it?" I asked him.
"What's *Celebrity Big Brother*, Patrick?" He asked.
I explained to him that you go into this big house and live there for a month with a load of other celebrities. You just have to be yourself. You wear a microphone, there are cameras everywhere and they watch, film and listen to you all the time you're there. Then each week the television viewers at home vote for one person to be evicted. After a moment's thought, and with a deeply troubled look on his face, he replied, "Don't do it, son."

I reasoned that I had already been portrayed by the press as a hard man and a bit of a terror and that this was an opportunity for me to show the public the other side of me and let them make up their own minds. I'd been made to look pretty good on *Danny Dyer's Deadliest Men* at first but I think they also took the mickey a bit, like I was a bit of a joke. I asked my wife, Roseanne.

"Don't do it, Paddy," she said. She told me if it all went wrong and I made a fool of myself, then I would make every Traveller look stupid too and they'd blame me for it. She had a point.

Eventually, I decided that it was a gamble I was prepared to take. I like risks, I always have, it's the way I'm built.

"All right then, my Paddy," Roseanne said, smiling and squeezing my hand, "go for it."

That's the thing about my Roseanne, she says her piece but then regardless of the decisions I make, she backs me up one hundred percent. She is my life.

So, I finally agreed and went in. As a Traveller myself, I thought everyone hated us – peoples' impression of us was that we were all trouble. I really believed at the time that only about one percent of people would be sympathetic to the Travellers, so I thought I might last one weekend in there and then get kicked out. I was stupid like that.

As it turns out, much to my surprise, I won. I really wasn't expecting that at all, no more than that a man could set foot on the moon.

After I'd won, people would say to me, "Oh, you did all right there, Paddy - a nice hundred grand for that," but in the end I was so embarrassed about it because I only received about thirty grand. I didn't know, however, that I would have to pay tax on that and that there would be all sorts of other expenses. It was a whole new world to me, I just thought that a clear thirty grand was mine and in my pocket, but of course it wasn't – but more of that later.

I was grateful to have made some good friends too while on *Celebrity Big Brother*, none more so than Sally Bercow, the wife of the then Speaker of the House of Commons (now former). Even though she was the first to be evicted, we just connected and got on as it were. This led to us working together on a variation of the *Wife Swap* television series called *When Paddy Met Sally* and then later, on *Paddy and Sally's Excellent Gypsy Adventure*.

## *Friends*

I remember when I came out of *Celebrity Big Brother,* I needed
a good break for a while, to get away and think about things.
This was about six months after *Celebrity Big Brother* and the
numerous, other TV appearances and some of the media
were doing what they usually do to create their stories, which
draw people in. Focusing in on the latest person who seems
to be doing well after a little dip into the world of 'celebrity' –
they start dragging me down, dredging up stuff from my past,
saying bad things about me all the time. It was really getting
to me and Roseanne and became too much to cope with. We
needed to get away from it all, away from the media hounding
us all the time. I had no idea where we could go, to escape for
a little while.

I realise now of course, but not at the time, that I was
hurtling towards a major breakdown. Every single newspaper
and magazine, and everywhere I turned, it seemed they were
saying things about my life, how it was out of control and
how I had become paranoid by the lies and all the media
exposure. They were absolutely right though, I was
unravelling, all because of them. I had no privacy at all, it felt

that my life was owned by someone else, everyone else apart from me and they made up so many stories and lies. I know they do it to get great headlines, notoriety and accolades, but at who's expense? Mine! My frame of mind! My family! True or not, why should it be plastered all over the place? I know being a celebrity puts you in the public eye, but why not for the good things? You know, like the charity work or the entertainment value and love for my family?

I have known Tracy for more than thirty years now and her husband Peter for more than twenty. Me and Roseanne love them dearly, they are a great couple and just lovely, loyal friends. You would never have thought that a Countryman and woman would be friends with Travellers and treat us so kindly. I love Tracy like a sister, she is a very kind woman with a lovely husband and son. They both knew me well enough to see the signs and realise that the pressure was getting to me and that I needed to get away for a little while. So, Tracy and Peter invited me and Roseanne to stay at their gorgeous home they had built in Cyprus, a big villa, to give us both some space and time to recover.

I remember having a great time, walking every day on the

beach, going out on the jet ski, holding hands and being like sixteen-year-olds again. It was so good just to be us and to be free of all the pressure.

We hardly touched any drink and would quite often go off on the scooter, riding around the island enjoying each other and the views. Roseanne would be on the back and Tracy and Peter would often come along on another scooter that they had, it was sheer bliss.

We took these scooters up into the mountains, just wonderful sights to be seen, so serene and blissful, a quiet paradise to us at that time. I used to love my time alone with Roseanne, watching the sun setting on the horizon, beautiful warming and relaxing colours, bleeding across the sky, made all the more spectacular being seen from the top of the mountain. It truly felt like we were in Heaven, we would just sit there. I felt like a young man, a young couple going out with each other for the first time, it was just lovely to see the joy in her eyes and the relaxed way she and I felt about each other once more.

It was like even though we were already in love of course, it felt like we fell totally back in love once again – paradise made real. All my worries went away, all my troubles with the media and the trapped feelings in my head, completely evaporated.

My good friends, Tracy and Peter, did not tell a soul that we were in Cyprus, no one, proper loyal friends both. So, we had two weeks of peace and bliss. Every morning I would get up real early and go for a three or four mile walk in the hills, just me and the birds, nature and peace – no cameras, or microphones waiting to trip me up.

There was a tiny church that I would often pass by on my walks, a small little chapel right in the middle of the hills, in the middle of nowhere. I would go inside and just sit there for ten or twenty minutes, chat to God and say a few prayers to my loved ones and ask God to mind me and watch over me.

With all this rest and peace, I started to feel a little stronger every day. Each day after my walk I would go in the pool that they had, sheer bliss, a paradise, I never thought I might be lucky enough to feel. The beach was just glorious and only a short walk away from their stunning villa.

We actually went to Cyprus with them four times in all and I will never ever stop thanking them both for helping me and Roseanne. Tracy is such a dear heart to me and Roseanne. As I said she is like my sister and Roseanne feels exactly the same way about her and she loves Peter like a big brother as well. Their son feels like one of my own too and he is Tracy's pride and joy her only son, and a lovely, lovely, young man with it. He has his own child now God bless him.

If you could ever wish for finer friends in the world just take a look at me, a third rate Traveller gypsy, I never thought I would be so lucky as to find two great friends like these two, just amazing people and I mean that from the bottom of my heart, I hope you are lucky enough to have good friends like that too.

Friends like that you have to be so lucky to get in a lifetime and I got blessed. A great Countryman and woman who loves us for who we are as people, not what we are or what background we have come from. They knew us through and through and understood us as just normal people, way before any of the fame and celebrity. True friends are there at the beginning and will be with you at the end.

They both have good business heads too. They have opened a bar in Manchester, called 'New York, New York' that caters to all people. All walks of life, all sexualities or gender people want to identify with, any colour any creed, all are welcomed with no judgement. They are humble, do not hold themselves above anyone else's walk in life, just good, kind people with open minds and hearts. All the tough nuts from Manchester meet up there because there is never any trouble whatsoever. They just will not tolerate any of it so it's a great place to be and feel safe at any time. It's a place where I would go and would never be disturbed, just a nice quiet drink and the ability to be myself and that's how it is for anyone that goes there. The bar is a clean, respectable, great place with no drugs, absolutely free of them. If you are ever there in Manchester and want a good welcome, call in and say hello to them both from me!

Some people think Sally Bercow is a bit of a snob, but she's not, not when you really get to know her, far from it. She's such a well-spoken woman, a tall woman, extremely well-mannered and educated but a real pleasure to be with. Having had the experience we had on that programme *When Paddy Met Sally*, Sally Bercow, until the end of my time, will be a dear, dear friend of mine.

I know, in my heart and soul as well, I will always be just the same to her, not sure about the husband mind you! I can't pretend I'm in love with him, he knows it all and everyone else knows nothing; at least that's how it felt some of the time, then again, he does know a lot. Some people say that might be his downfall. Some people say he knows everything but really knows nothing. But that's how intelligent he thinks he is, but he's a nice little fellow on the whole, so I can't really slag him off.

One thing I would say, is how blessed he is, to have got Sally Bercow and have her as his wife. They have three lovely children, two boys and one girl and they're absolutely three little angels. The little girl is like a mini beauty queen, she's absolutely bonny, out of this world. She's the image of her mother and the two boys are good-looking lads as well. They didn't follow John for their height because they are tall, where John is a little on the short side! Sally's life is their children and I have to say that would be the same for John too. He might have been the Speaker of the House and have this big political career, but above all else, he was a family man and to me he just loved and cared for his kids and his family. You could see he loved Sally with all his heart and I could see she loved him too. I hope they will always be happy, like me and Roseanne.

I made so many friends over the years, true friends and a very good friend of mine, Paul Mullins, a country chap. Some say he is a gangster and that he lives in that world and the Mullins's: Micky, Mark, Johnny Mullins, their old Daddy Tommy, all dear, dear friends of mine.

I have known Micky Mullins since I was a nipper. We knocked about together as kids and did everything together. His dear old Mummy, God rest her and save her, was a true lady.

Then, there was Tommy Turner, a lovely man indeed. Me and him did a lot of work together back in Ireland and over here. I worked with him on the *Gypsy Singing Contest* and it was great fun. This involved Travellers showing off their singing skills and me and Tommy organised it all. What a pleasure it was to see such enormous talent. It took a great deal of work, venues, security, hospitality. Finding, organising and catering to the competitors, took a lot of effort too, but I was real proud of this because it allowed the Travellers to be recognised for their special talents and skills.

Another friend of mine is Daniel Coll who organised this book, me and Dan went all over Japan together when we filmed the *Dan and Paddy's Bucket List* programme. He is a lovely guy; he has one daughter and is divorced now.

I have lots of country people friends these days. Good and bad, just like it is in the Traveller world.

## _When Paddy Met Sally_

I did a show called _When Paddy Met Sally_ with Sally Bercow, wife of the then Speaker of the House of Commons. Sally had been a fellow contestant in _Celebrity Big Brother_ and I knew that me and Sally would be good friends forever. She saw me as a kind, protective figure. That's how we became so close because I looked out for her on _Celebrity Big Brother_. I know many people saw it as an unlikely friendship, bizarre even, but we just clicked. I think it was because we were very much alike – fiery, outspoken and domineering. I saw Sally as this woman from the other side of the river, you know like she was from the posh and I was not! But we actually had a lot of experiences in common such as the drinking, depression and prejudice. I still to this day love to hear her speaking, I love her accent and how she pronounces words, just fascinating. After winning _Celebrity Big Brother_, Sally gave me a guided tour of Westminster which was brilliant. It was during that tour that Sally came up with the idea of doing another show with me about the Traveller community or a kind of celebrity _wife swap_.

One thing I will never forget is going to stay at Sally and John's apartment in Westminster for a memorable weekend with my wife Roseanne. This was because Sally had promised to give me a guided tour of the Houses of Parliament. Now, this is the truth and if Sally reads this, she will back me up one hundred percent. Sally told me that someone had warned them before our visit, "Hey, you want to hide the cutlery you know, if you've got them staying, they'll probably steal them!" Imagine saying we will steal a knife and fork, who do these people think we are? More to the point, who do they think they are, tarring us with the stereotypical, thieving gypsy personas. Just unbelievable. When she told me that I started laughing at first, I laughed it off like it was nothing. I can put a mask on and appear that I'm not bothered, but it really hurt, it truly hurt my heart. I thought to myself the people who said that were just cheeky tramps. It was only a couple of people of course but nevertheless, it hurt and I will never forget it.

The visit to the Houses of Parliament was so brilliant. It started with me and Sally arriving in the carpark at the back of the buildings. We were walking towards the Houses and there were a load of MPs milling around, well until they spotted us of course. It's funny now, they were just staring at us with shocked or disgusted facial expressions as if to say, "Look who we have here, look at this, look who is in our back yard, this can't be right, can it?"

Well, I just sniggered and I enjoyed it, walking with my head held high as if to say back,

"Yes, look at me. I am a Traveller and I am on your turf, stick that in your pipe and smoke it – Ha-ha!"

Sally was the same, she was enjoying showing them that she was more than happy to be in my company and that they could just 'do one', she was proud to be able to show me round and not care what anyone else thought.

We were given a tour of the formal state rooms of the Speaker's House, a magnificent apartment not open to the public and which can only be visited by invitation of the Speaker. The lush, crimson walls are covered with portraits of all the previous speakers, posing and dressed up in their fancy clothes and robes – there's one of John just dressed in his simple black gown as if he's working, standing in front of his chair in the House of Commons. The apartment was lavishly furnished with loads of fancy stuff and as well as a really impressive chandelier, there was a big red bed that the King or Queen would use the night before their coronation.

I was told no one was allowed on that bed. Well naturally, I had to jump on it. There was a barrier all the way around but that didn't stop me – I leapt over the barrier and jumped on the bed. It was great fun and we both had a good laugh. Sally told me afterwards that the last person to sleep in that bed was King George III. So don't tell anyone I did that, will you? We had a riotous time together!

I tell you what, Sally's a true truth good friend, she'll always be a friend to the day I die. I respect her and so does my wife and I also like her husband John very much but I definitely, really, really like Sally Bercow! She's a nice lady and she'll always be a lady in my eyes; a lady now and a lady till she dies.

After the visit to parliament I came back home and I was feeling on top of the world, happy, at the very top of my pedestal, as one would say. The very next day the media were on to me and it tortured me because they really thought, you know, we will have a bit of him but that's what it's like being a gypsy.

Sally and I were enjoying great craic together on *When Paddy Met Sally* and then suddenly the accusations that we were having an affair flared up in the press. I swear on my son's grave that nothing like that was going on, but the press wouldn't have any of it – they just carried on with their fantasies. At the same time, Sally was facing the same accusations from her husband's political party, not John himself, he knew there was nothing going on, but that didn't stop his 'pals' in parliament having a go.

The show though, seemed to go down well and the media ran with it and built me up so high it was unbelievable. Just crazy how high. It seemed I was being mentioned in the papers, on the radio or on TV every single day. It was like being as high as a skyscraper, like being on a crazy merry go round of a dream and I really didn't want to wake up. I DID NOT WANT TO WAKE UP! I was at the top and couldn't go any higher; it was as if I were Muhammed Ali, or President Reagan or the great Winston Churchill. Like being at the top of your game, indestructible, the greatest happy trip you could ever imagine. Except this wasn't a game or a dream, it was real.

Little did I know that I was soon going to dive off that skyscraper, and land, not in a shimmering pool, but on to pure concrete, headfirst with no crash helmet. That's one bad crash. I had no idea that it would have such an effect on my life and almost ruin it. Now, thank God, I have my life back and I'm better now than I ever was, but at the time, the depression really burned me up and to make things worse, an investigation by Her Majesty's Revenue and Customs followed.

## Celebrity Bainisteoir - The Rivals: Croke Park

One time, I went back to Ireland to do a show with Calum Best. I remember when I first met him, I did not know who I was going to be working with and I thought to myself, 'I know him from somewhere,' just such a familiar face to see.

So, Calum was sat amongst a whole group of other celebrities and I met him and got chatting having a craic. He was so arrogant and cocky it seemed to me.
"He is one cocky so-and-so," I remember saying to one of the producers of the show I was doing at the time, but I still did not know who it was.

We were on set one day to shoot, it may have been the first day of shooting and the director asks Calum, "Can you take your hat off?" in a real polite way.
Straight away Calum snaps back, "No, I won't," he said, in a real arrogant, full of himself, sort of way.
So, I went over to him and said, "He is only asking you to take your hat off for a better shot."
"I won't take it off for no one," said Calum.

I have to say, at that point, I really felt like hitting this fella for disrespecting the director in this way. He had the look and feel of a tough man, but I knew that you could break him up in seconds. It felt to me that if he was a bar of chocolate, he would eat himself. We did, in the end, become good mates as it happens but at the time these were my impressions.

The point of this program was that we were making was about a Gaelic football tournament and my team to work with was Dublin. Now I swear to God, I had never seen Gaelic football before but in a nutshell, I had to manage the team from Dublin. These players were all amateurs but the truest professionals ever; a great bunch of hard-working lads; wonderful players and a great craic. I got on great with them all. Calum's dad of course, was George Best, *THE* bees' knees, the best. So, time goes on in the filming of this programme and slowly Calum starts to grow on me.
I remember one day saying to him, "Why are you so arrogant, so cocky, to all the other people?" and he opened up to me, respect to him.
He said, "Paddy, I have been hurt that many times by producers and suchlike and sometimes they have cut

everything in such a way to make a laughingstock of me, so now I am just worried over everyone I meet."

At that point I knew what he meant. He had been damaged by them and was trying to protect himself in the best way he knew how and who can blame him for that in the end?

I said to him, "I thought you were an arrogant so-and-so at first," and he started laughing out loud. This was a real warm laugh at himself, not a snigger in any way, just a true, honest, healthy laugh at life. After that point we really started to get on and work well together.

So, we carried on filming and each team is knocking others out in the games and finally it came to me and Calum's teams time to play each other. I have to say even though Dublin, my team, were brilliant, they did in fact lose to Calum's in the end, after a really close game.

When it came to the final, Calum's team were in the play and lo and behold, his team won that too. Now that had to make him the top man in the end, the true bees' knees, earned this time in the end. It was okay, I guess, as my team had been beaten by the best so all's well that ends well!

That evening, we were all having a beer in the hotel and I remember saying to everyone that I had to get off and I found myself in the lift with Calum.

He said to me, "Ah, don't go yet Paddy, let's have a bit more fun."

I told him I might join him later and he went back down to the bar. In the end, I eventually fell asleep and left the drinking to the others.

In the morning I saw Calum at the breakfast table, so I joined him, there was just me and him.

"You know what Paddy? You're a true, honest and good friend," he said to me.

"You know what Calum, I didn't like you at first, I thought you were arrogant and cocky, but you are really far from that in truth! In actual fact, you're a gentleman and you have been hurt by too many people," I said back to him.

"You know what Paddy? You're a real, true, good friend of mine from now on in!"

I can read people and their body language and I knew he was speaking the truth and that we had made a great connection. I can honestly say that I now feel blessed to know Calum Best as a friend and also a nice man. He is someone who has had it a little tough and I really wish him all the best in the world and I hope he finds the right woman to find happiness with. I am smiling to myself, thinking, he could do with a bold woman, a cheeky woman, a woman who would chastise him and keep him in line in a good way.

I remember getting home and speaking to Roseanne, who was asking about the filming and the like.
"What was Calum like?" She asked, and I was telling her all about him and how really, underneath it all, he was the nicest chap, nicest young fella in the world.

In time, Calum came to my home and spent a few days with me, it was a sheer pleasure, we had a few drinks together and spent some good times. Let me tell you, the young women and some not so young, were like bees around a honey pot but he didn't seem to notice at all and we just had a wonderful time together, great fella and lovely man. I felt so honoured that he came down and spent a good few days with me, that is what you call a true friend, who followed up on his word to come and spend some time with me. So, what you see with Calum is what you get, no airs or graces, pure honesty, just him, the best of men (no pun intended).

I bet you didn't know that there was a famous Irish Gaelic footballer call Paddy Doherty, did you? He was from Ballykinlar and he captained the Mournemen when they retained the All-Ireland SFC title in 1961.

He was one of the greatest forwards in the history of the game. Some of his exploits, his confidence on the field, his abilities, were unbelievable. He and his team changed football; they changed the whole course of the game.

I can't get over how truly wonderful Ireland is. It's an amazing country, just a stunning place to go to, with the nicest of people. I would love my children to go back for a while, three of them have had a couple of days there.

## _Paddy and Sally's Excellent Gypsy Adventure_

Sally is very, very dear to me and the respect I have for her is on a different level. She is a lovely lady all the way round. Sally is a nice lady to look at, a nice lady to speak to, and she has a heart as big as the world, she has a great heart. A lovely woman in every way and always.

So, me and Sally were asked to do another TV programme called _Paddy and Sally's Excellent Gypsy Adventure_. I remember when we were making the documentary, me and Sally, we went what felt like all over the world to do it. We actually went to Ireland to get a feel for my origins and then to Spain to spend some time with the Spanish gypsies.

So, Ireland then… The respect we got in Ireland was just mind blowing and I really couldn't believe it, being a Traveller. I never thought, and I don't mean this in a disrespectful way, that Irish people would be so supportive and friendly towards Travellers. They couldn't do enough for us and the Irish people were honestly, just so kind to me and Sally, it blew my mind. When you add all the time together in my life up to that point, I'd only spent about six weeks in

Ireland and most of that was in Dundalk or Dublin. So, the longest I've ever spent in Ireland in one go, was when I made *Paddy and Sally's Excellent Gypsy Adventure* and we filmed that over a week, it was just amazing, fantastic, truly, truly breath-taking.

When we were making this programme, we went to different parts of Ireland. I remember going to a fair, a place where the beautiful Irish actress Maureen O'Hara came from, God rest her soul. She was in that film with John Wayne, *The Quiet Man*. I forget the county it was in because the whole time we were filming, we were running around all over the place, so fast, but I'd heard she would be coming to where we were the very next day.

I was so excited, I was like, "Maureen O'Hara, she's coming here, I love that woman, just amazing, I love that woman so much!"

At that time, she was well into her eighties, maybe more but I didn't care. I was like a little boy, having seen her in *The Quiet Man* and lots and lots of other films like *Miracle on 34th Street*, *Rio Grande*, *Big Jake* and *The Parent Trap*, as a kid, I was just in awe of her. Now, we had to leave the next day to carry on filming and I went to the director and I begged him, I said,

"Please, please, can we stay here just one more day? Oh my, Oh my, Mummy please? I'll do anything you want. I'll work harder…" I was just begging this director for the chance to meet my screen idol.

The director looked at me; I couldn't tell what he was thinking and then suddenly a big smile breaks over his face and he said, "Okay, Paddy, we'll do that for you my man, we will do that for you."

I was in the stars, like a little schoolboy who'd been given the best present of all time. It turns out we were in the same hotel and we waited, I waited, all the next day getting more and more nervous. I went for a little jog for a few miles to try and break some of the tension. I came back, looking around, asking around, to see if Maureen O'Hara had arrived, I was like a bold child desperate for a sweet. I went to bed that night and I couldn't sleep; I was like a child waiting for Christmas morning to open his presents. The next morning, I flew down the stairs because the lift was too slow, I was that desperate to see her. I asked where she was and the director looked at me and said,

"I'm really sorry, buddy, it doesn't look like she's gonna be here."

It turned out she wasn't coming till later that day and we had to go, I couldn't hold the crew up any longer, it was time to move on and do some more filming in another part of Ireland.

As you're driving along, I remember thinking what a beautiful country it was. I was reflecting and had turned my mind inwards, very quiet, miles away, just alone with my thoughts. That kind of environment, the peace, the tranquillity, the beauty, lends itself to quiet, isolated reflection. At that time, nobody really knew about all the problems I'd been having or the state of my nerves, but Sally did, she's a very clever lady and tuned in. She got to know me well and know all my moves and ways, she knew how I was feeling almost more than I did. At that point, most people thought everything was fine. I was great with people and having a laugh, being myself and being the big man, then suddenly I'd go dark and grey in colour, go downhill and go very quiet, I just needed to get away.

Sally, bless her heart, out of the blue, would say,

"Oh Paddy, I just want a quiet word with you. Let's go for a little walk," and off we would go, to get away from everybody for a few moments.

We'd both go off walking away just for twenty minutes, half an hour or so. Sally would sit down and have a cigarette, puffing away quietly and then she would say,

"How are you feeling now Paddy, a little bit better?"

"Sorry, how did you know I was feeling a bit rough?" I said back.

With a big smile on her face, she turned to me and said,

"Paddy, I know everything!"

I said to Sally, "Okay, thank you so much for looking out for me and looking after me. It's funny that you just knew when I wasn't feeling right." She did it millions of times, to make me feel better, what a lady.

Thanks Sally if you're reading this. She was like my wife, my wife always knew when I was in one of those moods, she was so sensitive. The problem was, I wasn't on any medication at that time, but I guess I didn't really realise I needed it that much.

Another time, I remember Sally turning to me with a big smile on her face as we were sitting together again and she said to me, "Are you seeing a doctor Paddy? Are you talking to anybody? Are you working it through?"

I said, "Of course I am silly, I've been seeing somebody."

"Well, are you taking any medication, anything to help you?" She asked.

I told her that I did have something, that the doctor had prescribed some tablets for me. The problem was, when I said this to her, I was lying, I wasn't actually on any medication at the time and over two or three days, the guilt began to get to me because she didn't deserve to be lied to, for being such a caring woman.

Well sure enough I had another black time a few days later and again, Sally says,

"Come on, let's go for a walk."

So off we trot. She waited until we had walked quite far away from everyone else and she started to ask me again about the medication and stuff and in the end, I had to cut her off mid-sentence and confess my lie to her.

I said, "Sally, please don't think bad of me, please – when I said I was seeing a doc and getting help and medication, I wasn't, please don't be mad at me, I'm not on any medication, I'm sorry."

"I knew, I knew it!" She said to me, with a massive smile on her face and I couldn't help but smile back.

"I knew it Paddy," she said again, "look," putting her hands on my shoulders, "you've got to go and get help with this. Go and speak to someone Paddy, a professional. There's no shame in it, no one else need know about it anyway but you must go see your doctor, get some help, get some medication, okay?"

So, I told her, no I promised Sally that when we got back home, I'd go and see somebody and I'd get the help. I couldn't carry on like that anymore, I felt like I was going out of my mind.

But the questioning didn't end there, like a dog with a bone Sally asked me what Roseanne would say or think about the situation and I knew I couldn't lie about it, so I told her, "My poor Roseanne doesn't know whether she's coming or going with me at the moment, I am so up and down all the time, but it's great that I can talk to you Sally, you're a stranger, Roseanne is my wife and I just don't want to hurt her. She's been through so much pain in her life already, it's just a big mess."

Sally looked me in the eye, held my hands and said, "Tell Roseanne everything, and I mean everything!"

"But I don't want her to get worried about me, I don't want to add to her already fragile situation and make her feel worse than she does right now." I said.

"That is what she's there for," she says, "to worry about you, the same as you worry about her. You worry about your woman and, by the way," she says to me, with an even bigger smile on her face, "I hate you calling her woman!"

I said, "Sally, that's just men and our culture. It's used a lot by men in our culture, we've always called our wife, 'my woman'. We don't mean or cause any harm by it. Our women don't even notice it or take offense at it. It's like Countrymen calling their wives 'my better half' or 'her indoors'. From the age of sixteen she's always been 'my woman' nobody else's, just mine."

"Well just you make sure you tell her, okay?" Sally said. Thinking back now on that conversation, I felt a bit lighter, thinking I may just be able to do something about this problem at last.

That night, we were supposed to sleep in a wagon or a tent, you know, to soak up the culture and feel like we were true Travellers, even though I'd done it many times, it was a new situation for Sally to find herself in.

"So, my sister Sally, are you sleeping in the tent with me then?"

She turned around and said to me, "I'm not sleeping in no tent, no way, I'm staying in a hotel!"

I was a bit surprised, I thought she might try it out, but it looks like it was just one step too far for her into the world of the true Traveller – Ha-ha! So, I said to her,

"Well, if you're doing that, then I'm staying in a hotel too!" And we both roared with laughter.

Me and Sally had such fun on that programme and it was the people of Ireland that made it that way, the people. I've been lucky enough to travel to quite a few places and there is nothing quite like Ireland itself. It's the way they use the language and the slang, the way they tell a tale and embrace new people, the most welcoming country of all countries. As we travelled further along and deeper into the countryside, the people seemed to get friendlier, just unbelievable.

One of my biggest shocks was how popular I was in Ireland and well known I was. I just didn't know, I had no idea it was that way, that people knew me like they did. Another good thing about the Irish people is that they treat you just like you are one of them, like in their family or something, so as well as being well known, they treat you normal, they treat you with respect, they gave me such respect, I was humbled and I gave and still give that respect back in spades.

After Ireland, me and Sally went to Spain, but I couldn't tell you which part of Spain it was, I just know that we had a really good time! This was to meet the Spanish gypsies and see how much like the UK Travellers they were or weren't.

I have never seen anything like it in my life! They weren't in trailers and such like, a lot of them lived in houses and when I say houses, I mean spectacular houses. Even so, you would know they were Travellers the minute you set eyes on them. As a people they were really dark skinned, their homes were out of this world. They were very protective over Sally; they didn't seem to like Sally being in the house with them and the men. The Spanish gypsies don't believe a woman is above the man, so I would say they found her a bit of a challenge.

I remember being sat with the main man of the group, he was Spanish and I was English of course, but somehow, I could understand everything he was saying and he could definitely understand me. We had an immediate, strong connection and a way of communicating with each other that I can't explain. It was just unbelievable how we understood one another so clearly. Of course, the camera crew were all there and this chap says to me,

"Paddy, I would like for you to come to our wedding in three days' time."

"I would love to!" I said. A full-on, proper Spanish Wedding. He said to me, "You're going to see things there that you would never have seen before anywhere in the world."

I said, "Yeah, yeah, sounds good to me, I can't wait." Now I am thinking to myself, this is just a normal wedding, or will it be like one of ours, where family pride comes into it and they need to be bigger and better than the last?

He said to me, "I will pick you up at the hotel."

Sally says with a big posh smile, "Oh, that is jolly nice, we will go together."

His wife-to-be somehow knew and had worked out what Sally was saying. She glanced over at her husband-to-be and gave him 'the look', then she looked me right in the eye, and I knew she was silently telling us both a resounding 'NO'. Well, the man took a simple look at his wife-to-be and that look overruled her immediately to a YES!

So, a few days later me and Sally are getting ready for the wedding and I turned to her and said, "Now Sally, don't forget this is gypsies and Spanish gypsies at that. This is an entirely different culture to the way me and you work. They will be having a craic and lots of things will be going on that might surprise you or you might not understand, so don't be giving your opinion about anything, okay? Because these are gypsies, true-traditional Travellers, what they say is law. They will not welcome or understand your opinion and may even take offense at it. I'm not saying this to upset you or because I don't value your opinion, I do, but just be aware of this and try your best, please."

"Yeah Paddy, yeah Pad, yeah, don't worry," she replied. There she goes again calling me 'Pad' when she knows I hate that name.

Following the meeting with the 'housed' Spanish gypsies we moved on to visit with the 'Sea Gypsies'. I was shocked and curious at the same time. These 'Sea Gypsies' lived in boats on the actual sea! Unbelievable! At first, I found it hard to believe, but their houses were on stilts, boat houses on stilts. I have to say it was the strangest thing to see. I remember one evening we were there in one of these houses on legs and there was a couple there just having sex while people were walking around or by them! This would seem odd to us but in their lifestyle, it was perfectly normal and people seemed to just accept it as the norm – it was a really strange experience. I remember being in total shock, I just could not believe this was happening, at the same time I couldn't stop laughing as it was so bizarre perfectly normal to them but just WOW!

I remember needing to go to the toilet and not for a pee! Of course, there was no toilet, it was just a hole in the floor of a room, which was open to the sea below it, a bit like it would have been back in Elizabethan times I guess, it was so backwards, like we'd stepped back in time. No toilet paper either! What you had to do was dip your bum into the sea and give it a good wash, some might say it was a cleaner way to do it. I finished my poo and I went back into the other room and there's this couple in the corner just banging away as if it was totally normal.

I remember going to sleep because I was really tired with all this madness going on around me and the sea was bashing against the sides of the house (if you could call it that).

The next morning Sally appears, "Oh, Hi Paddy," she said, bright as a bobbin.

I started to tell her the whole story about everything I had seen and about the experience of using the open-air toilet, which was weird enough on its own, but even weirder was the way people were just strewn around the floor sleeping, seemingly oblivious or blind to the couple making love in the corner.

"No way!" she said, laughing out loud and grinning from ear to ear. "I don't believe it," she continued with her mouth hanging open in a big 'O'. She then covered her mouth with her hand in embarrassment.

"They were banging each other like rabbits I tell ya, I kid you not!"

"God, I wish I'd seen that. That's hilarious!" She said to me, rocking back and forwards,

"I wish I'd been there, damn!"

I told her how in the end, that I had to go and sleep in the veranda with the waves lashing over the top notch, "I just didn't know where to put myself!" I said.

She's smiling and still rocking back and forward, laughing even more. She said to me,

"Well, if it's so normal for them, you know, part of the culture and your Traveller culture, why didn't you just stay in there?"

I said, "Sally, I couldn't stay there and watch this young couple banging away all night, it's just not the sort of thing I'm in to!" She thought that was hilarious.

Later that day we went riding and then of course we spent some time with the bulls. These are the normal touristy type things people do when they visit Spain. It's great when you go to new places like this, you get to see and do things you've never done before. You might have seen it on TV and it looks exciting, spectacular, scary, but to actually experience it yourself is amazingly and fantastically something else.

We were taken to do some spear fishing which was brilliant. You're looking down into the water through your snorkel mask and you can see hundreds of fish swimming around. Their colouring is like a rainbow before your eyes, or like a kaleidoscope flashing as the fish turn and the sun catches their scales. It's strange in a way, because until you actually look down into the water, you don't even realise they are there, swimming around you, going about their fishy business. Anyway, we were filming underwater, spotting the fish and trying to spear them. The spears were sharp but the handle or poles felt quite flimsy, you know, bendy and when you aim the spear and let it go, it would veer off and completely miss the fish. It took a while to get used to that, so I personally didn't spear many, but it was great fun and you didn't realise how the time flew by.

Well, I say it was great fun and it was, until Sally got stung by this gigantic, ugly-looking jellyfish. I was oblivious to what was going on, so intent was I on the fish spearing. The crew described what had happened. The first thing they saw was Sally's head coming out of the water. She was making this noise somewhere between a scream and a gurgle, trying to spit out the snorkel mouthpiece. Her face was contorted into a visage of absolute distress and agony. She was screaming and shouting and carrying on.

The crew were shouting, "What is it? What's wrong with the woman? What's wrong Sally?"

"OH, BAD, BAD, BAD, OH MY GOD, OH, OW, OW, OW!" She's screaming and shouting. Her arms are flapping about as if she were drowning. She was screaming my name; she was screaming her husband John's name.

She was in a proper panic, "I CAN'T STAND THIS, I CAN'T BEAR IT ANYMORE, I CAN'T BEAR THIS," she's screaming, "I HAVE TO GET AWAY FROM IT!" The next minute, the crew grab hold of Sally and throw her into the dinghy boat and I'm still diving with the Sea Gypsies trying to spear and kill the fish. So, I'm carrying on with the filming I go down and I try and kill a few more fish. The next time I surface, I can't see Sally anywhere, so I asked the crew where she was and that's when they told me she was in the boat and that she'd been really, really badly stung and they'd have to take her back to land.

"No way!" I said and now I was really worried.

So, the next thing I find myself swimming over to the boat and I finally get there and it's too high for me to get myself out of the water. I managed to get my head just over the edge and could peep into the boat and see Sally.

"Oh, my lovely Sally, how are you? Are you all right?" I said to her.

"No, I'm not all right, Paddy!" she screamed at me, crying and really upset, "I've been badly stung!"

For the rest of the day, all she did was moan and complain. Understandable I guess in the circumstances, but still a pain in my backside.

There was this little, old woman sitting on the shore, I swear, she looked about five hundred years old. You could tell she'd had a hard life, a working life of a sea gypsy. She was a deep, deep brown, sun-wrinkled skin, but she still had a twinkle in her eye. The lady could not speak a word of English, but she knew Sally was upset just from the way she was carrying on and luckily, we had an interpreter there. This little sea gypsy woman looks over at me and winks and as I said, she certainly looked two hundred if not five hundred years old. The wink was as if to say from one Traveller to another, 'I'm going to shut this woman up now because all she's doing is going on and on and on.' Now when she winked at me, I didn't really cotton on to what she was obviously thinking at the time. She babbles something to the interpreter, pointing at Sally and moving her arm up and down to cover the area where Sally had been stung.

"The old lady says you've got to piss into this bucket," the interpreter says to Sally. Sally looked at him with disbelief in her eyes and raised her eyebrows.

"What? I've got to wee into that? You've got to be kidding me!"

The old lady nods with absolute sincerity, with a slight glint in her eye.

"Piss into the bucket and pour it over the wound where you were stung." The interpreter continued.

God forgive me, but I couldn't stop laughing my head off! I'm in the sea bobbing up and down with the waves and rocking backwards and forwards laughing at the same time, peeping into the boat, seeing Sally and this old lady glaring at each other. I just couldn't stop laughing. The sight of Sally, a well-educated, well-spoken, well-mannered woman, this five-hundred-year-old sea gypsy woman and myself in this mad situation, was too much for any man. I was rocking backwards and so much with laughter I thought I was going to drown.

I'm not being disrespectful to Sally, or any woman, nor am I a dirty minded man, I promise you, far from it, but I have to say it, Sally was wearing this ultra-tight, sexy costume.

"How on earth are you going to take the costume off and have a piss right here with all of us around?" I asked Sally but she didn't answer me. She just looked at me and rolled her eyes.

The next minute, I had to look away because, beggar me, Sally was there pulling the bottom part of the costume over to one side and finding the bucket. I turned my head away and hears her pissing into the bucket. Well, I was roaring with laughter so much so that I started to swallow water, just could not control myself and I have to say quite a few other crew members were having a laugh too. I looked over to see the camera man with the camera pointing at her, but even so he was laughing his head off too and the sound man was shaking so much, he could barely keep the boom still, it was hilarious! Poor old Sally, I have to say she had a great sense of humour.

I looked back over at the old gypsy woman, the five-hundred-year-old gypsy woman and she had the biggest smile on her face, she winked at me and she's rocking back and forwards too and I realise what she's been up to. Great sense of humour that lady had! Sally poured the liquid over the sting wound and it did actually give her some relief. It hasn't put her off in the slightest, she still loves the water today. I have to say we got on so well did me and Sally and she was a joy to be with, what a story.

We got on so well in fact, that a lot of people, I'm sure were saying behind our backs to others that we must have been having an affair because of how well we got on. Well, I swear, we never ever did anything like that. We were just great mates. I swear on my God, nothing like that ever happened. I have to be honest, I never looked at Sally like that and I'm sure she felt the same about me we were just really good buddies. End of Story. Sally is just a lovely, lovely woman, she is just a good woman, a diamond and a great laugh. That's why Sally will always be my friend. We haven't seen each other for a little while but she's always in my mind and in my thoughts and I'm sure I will catch up with her soon, maybe when this book comes out. As I say, she's the lady of all ladies to me, great family, great children, great husband – lovely little man – just great.

At that time, I knew very little about the television game as they call it and Sally used to say to me, "Paddy, when you're talking to the press and the media, just say nice things about me and I'll be saying the same about you, really good things." I promised her that's what I would do and that's what I did do, when I talk to the media and the press, not sure it all worked out though. At the end of the series when we finished filming, I remember giving Sally a big kiss and a hug, it was a fantastic time. I was really surprised that there wasn't another series of *When Paddy Met Sally,* we had great fun making it and I know that the audience, from what I heard, enjoyed it too.

## *Work*

When I left school, I got out and I worked real hard to get nice things about me and feel good about myself. Eventually I bought a house, a real beauty of a house and the mad thing was I never ever lived in it.

I bought a new Bentley Continental GT. I was very wealthy at that point, bought my wife Roseanne a new Jeep, I got everything I ever wanted and needed materially in the world.

I remember the old schoolteacher had said to me, "You will be good for nothing! You will never make anything of yourself, Paddy Doherty."
Well, one day, I dressed superbly and I drove the car back to the school, parked outside and waited for him to leave so he could see it.
"Sir," I said, "My name is Paddy Doherty and I am good for nothing! That car there is mine! I've got my own house, bought and paid for and my wife has a Jeep!" I remember at that time just wanting to hurt this old teacher because he had always treated me real bad, like I was vermin or dirt under his shoe. I walked away and left the scent of my success in the

air. At that one point in my life, I needed to prove I was something to this man who had made my life Hell while at that particular school. His face was a picture that day, it made up for all the days gone by.

I remember picking up my car and on the same day four *United* players picked up theirs on that day. It was a special day, that day. I remember when I picked it up, I had had a real long, hard day at work and I was dressed like a tramp. I brought my brother Martin with me and said to him, "Here Martin, you drive the car out of the showroom." The surprise on his face was ace!
He said, "What?"
I said, "You drive it!" He was the first to drive my Bentley and the smile he had on him was just great.

I have nothing at the moment, in the realms of finance; one might say I am financially embarrassed, but it is what it is and life has a way of moving on. I had it, I had been there, I had done that and now it's gone!

So, during and after *Celebrity Big Brother*, I had an agent, you probably know who he actually was, but for the sake of propriety, let's call him 'Sausage'. I was in demand, I was there in 'Sausage's' office and people were calling him, asking for me to go places and make appearances, do interviews, charity work, the lot. 'Sausage' was having none of it though. One of the callers was asking me to go to Ireland to do a film, and without consulting me, 'Sausage' was saying no, turning the work down, I had no idea why.

I did not know it at the time, but 'Sausage' had been having arguments with some of these people in the past, professional quarrels, quarrels that had nothing to do with me but I felt it was me that had done something wrong, me that was causing trouble, or had done something wrong to 'Sausage' himself! I was at a loss to understand why. He just kept on saying no to them. It was absolutely nothing to do with me or anything I had done, but all I know is I lost a lot of work. There was a load of work requests coming in but I was not allowed to do the work, he just kept telling them no. Lost me a fortune!

Of course, what I should have done was to do it any way, but I simply thought I had to go through him, I was so green to how the business worked back then.

Well now, another dear, dear friend of mine, Darryn Lyons, an Australian, who I met on *Celebrity Big Brother*, had been trying and trying, a million times, to get in touch with me through my agent. My agent told me about this but said I wasn't allowed to associate with him, yet this was a close and dear friend of mine. I was so confused, but I trusted my agent, after all, they are the ones that are supposed to look after you, supposed to protect you from the media, supposed to find you lucrative work, supposed to make you successful and obviously share in that success, aren't they? I know I only knew Darryn from *Celebrity Big Brother*, but we sort of fell in love, you know like good friends, not love like you love your woman, I mean love like you have for a good, dear friend. He was a Countryman, with a bit of a wild reputation, but switched on, like experienced in this world of celebrity, larger than life, full of life and laughter, a media man, a politician and an entrepreneur, a businessman like me and we just clicked.

When we finally spoke, Darryn said to me, "You should be in the theatre now and you should be doing pantomimes and stuff like that."

So, I told my agent this, but he was adamant and told me that I couldn't do it.

He said to the room of people, "NO! We can't be having Paddy in a panto, absolutely not, he is a gypsy!"

Again, that really hurt because loads of people who did *Celebrity Big Brother* also did a few pantomimes, so how was that fair?

People discriminate against Travellers all the time and this was an example of that prejudice but in the worst way, from a person who was supposed to be helping you. It's not right; we all know this, but unfortunately, it's the way it still is in many ways.

I remember my agent phoning me one day and to my utter surprise, based on what had happened in the past, he said, "Would you like to switch on the Christmas lights in Blackpool?"

I was over the moon, ecstatic, and of course I said I would love to. But that was the first and last I heard about it, ultimately nothing ever came of it.

Then everything snowballed and I knew I was losing, I was losing major money, major, major money – working what felt like twenty-four by seven – but receiving very little for the work, for what I was doing. It was going somewhere but I was not seeing a lot of it.

The main trouble was, that my life was really mixed up at that time, I didn't know it at the time, it took like twelve to fourteen months to realise it but I was slowly having a breakdown, but I didn't see it.

One day my woman said to me, "Why don't you just get a new agent?" and I said, "Roseanne your right, I am going to do it, I am going to find myself a different agent."

As I said, I was very new to all this at the time and it's only lately I am getting to understand the way the business really works.

The best agent I ever found was Sharron of IEA Talent. She was the best agent ever, she was a diamond, a lovely, lovely woman, in London she was. She was a great lady, she had feelings, cared, you know, not just all cold and calculating and she looked after her clients, a nice woman to go with it and her staff were fantastic too.

She really started to look after me and got me parts in two movies: *Rise of The Footsoldier 3*, a film about the real-life events of the notorious gangster, Pat Tate and how he rises through the ranks of Essex's criminal underworld, battles rival drug dealers, vicious prison inmates and gets double-crossed by drug lord Frank Harris. My part was small and I played the head Traveller of a gypsy campsite. One of my boys had been accused of selling drugs in one of Pat's nightclubs and got a slap from one of his guys, falling over and cracking his head open, ended up in hospital. Pat came to see me at the campsite to apologise for him getting hurt and to make peace, call a truce, no retribution. We exchanged a few words and they showed Pat thinking about what could happen if the talks went south. The cut scene showed us grappling with each other and me biting his face. We shook hands, and I said, "Listen, on my boy's life, I've shook yer hand and this time it's water under the bridge right?" But then one of his lackies pipes up and annoys me and Pat has to smooth the way again. The best message at the end of the scene when one of Pat's lackies asked, "You going to trust the word of a fucking 'pikey'?" and Pat's response was, "Once they shake your hand, they never ever go back on their word!" And that is so true.

The second part was in a film called *Blackbird*, written and directed by the fantastic Irish dancer, Michael Flatly of *Riverdance* fame. His film was about a secret agent known as 'Blackbird' who retires to the Caribbean to escape his past, where he opens a nightclub, but trouble finds him again. My part again was small, but I heard tell that he'd specifically asked for me for this part. The scene is a boxing match where I am the trainer in the boxer's corner of the boxing ring and the bell for time out has rung, the boxer comes over and sits on his stool and I am coaching him, giving him tips on how to fight his opponent and giving him water and such like. I really enjoyed doing that – it was brilliant.

Everything just snowballed from there then. The media was after me every minute. The second I did anything slightly wrong in their eyes, they would expose it, pour the petrol and generally make things worse than they really were.

About twelve months down the line my wife took sick. I watched over her the best I could, her nerves were very bad, so I took care of her. I was doing the odd little thing here and there and trying to keep it steady, but it was just a bad period for me, I was really worried about Roseanne and couldn't concentrate on anything but her. That's when another family crisis hit us, all of a sudden, my daughter, Margaret, was having problems with her husband So the work obviously took a hit and had to slow down.

It's a funny thing since I wrote my first book, I thought to myself, 'This is it, it's all wonderful and everything is going to be fantastic in my life from this point onwards.' I remember having so much work it was unbelievable.

At one point I was working regularly and earning good money every day. So, I was thinking I've made millions, I am rich, it's all going to be great from this day forward and I will be secure.

Well, so not the case, of course! I lost everything I had. Every bit of extra money I had behind me was gone. I've only myself to blame – I got into gambling and casinos in a stupid and big way.

I lost the lot! I would not say I am broke now, as I still have my wife and my family around me; I have my life and I am all right you might say. There is an old saying, '*Not rich, not poor, but comfortable*'. I have to be honest, that's right where I am now and I am happy with life like that.

## *Being a Traveller*

Before I start sharing my thoughts and stories on being a Traveller, I want to take some time to explain what being a Traveller means, as the 'official' definition of a 'Traveller' is not clear-cut. You should know that it focuses on habitual lifestyle rather than ethnicity. I hope that by reading this and getting an understanding of the 'Travelling' way of life, you come to understand, tolerate and even cooperate with us better.

The first Irish Travellers were recorded in the eighth century as travelling metal workers and menders of household utensils. Our language is known as Cant or Gammon and we are mainly of the Catholic faith and prefer to send our children to Catholic schools. We have a shared culture, language and belief system.

You do not have to travel to be a Traveller! Historically maybe, but today and in the future not so much. Did you know that ninety percent of Travellers around the world now live in houses? Even though this is true, our culture and heritage stay with us.

Some groups of Travellers though, are still highly mobile, moving on when work opportunities have ended and others live permanently in one area or only travel for a few weeks or months of the year.

Most Traveller families live within close-knit communities, whether in housing or on caravan sites, with strong family and social networks. We use modern, good-quality vehicles and caravans. Our main reason for travelling is to work, follow fairs and visit family. Travelling patterns are linked to the seasons and the work associated with those seasons. We don't travel on a daily basis or all year round. Our families need safe and secure places from which to do our travelling. The 'base' site will usually be where we can easily access GPs, schools, hospitals and dentists.

Also, as Travellers grow older, they sometimes become less able to travel on a regular basis, and so need a safe and secure stopping place where they can maintain the cultural traditions of being a Traveller. We also sometimes stop travelling for periods of time to care for sick or elderly relatives or to continue our child's education within a supportive school environment. Families may then take up the travelling way of life again following these critical events.

I think of myself as Irish. I talk Irish, I act Irish, I think of myself truly as an Irish man, but my downfall is that I wasn't born in Ireland, I was born in Manchester, but I still think of myself as Irish as if I had been born there.

I love Ireland; I would die for Ireland, but I know I'm also British and so I also respect my country Britain. I would give my life for Ireland and since our visit to the 'Emerald Isle', I think Sally Bercow would also give her life, but I have to laugh as it wouldn't be for Ireland it would be for England "Ha-ha-ha!"

I think looking back one of the best parts of my life was when I was fifteen, I was so happy just before I left school, the only snag was, in those days you left school when you were fifteen, hard to believe when you look at it now. I really only went to school, given all the time I had missed, for a few years but I loved most of it, I loved my friends, Philip Boswell, Paddy Quail, Bradley Lincoln, Clive Wellington, who in fact became one of my brothers-in-law, dead now God rest his soul, all of them.

Life can be a funny old world, well not that it is funny, it's a sad life in so many ways yet good. When you're small you wish you were big and then when you get big you wish you were small because you don't realise that the best years of your life are really when you are small, young and at school.

School is possibly the greatest time in the world and if you are lucky enough to go to college then that is the icing on the cake. That is why I believe that for Travellers, education is more important than anything in the world! Every travelling child should be in school, I don't care who they are, what they are, race they are or what ways they have of living, every child should be at school and get an education. Education is the most important thing you can get to set you up for life.

A lot of Travellers miss out on education, particularly those of my generation, their parents didn't really appreciate how important this was for the child. In those days, the stick you got for being a Traveller when you went to school was bad and the parents thought they were protecting their kids by keeping them out, but it is changing now I would say, things are better for Travellers at school. There's still room for improvement but it is better now than it was in my time, that's for sure.

I used to just love it, spuds, cabbage and ribs, oh Mummy, which would be like caviar to me, it was the bees' knees, just perfect. Oh, and a loaf of bread with a pound of butter on it and a good bit of salt and pepper, I am jumping with joy just thinking about that meal now. To round it off, I would love to eat rice and jelly, no kidding, loads of it, I could eat it until the cows came home.

In fact, sometimes, old Christie and Winnie Joyce's sons would come over to ours to eat and then we would go over to theirs sometimes and we would get another great dinner off them. The family never called them Mummy and Daddy, it was always Mum or Dad. Normally you don't hear Travellers talking that way, but this family rated their mum and dad so much higher than anyone else. Mum and Dad is a very polite expression somehow in our community and that's how they were both known by their children, always.

Travellers are a very close-knit people, close to one another's families. We would always be going to each other's houses and eating really good food together, when we were given the chance.

Travellers are all together, like we are in a nest, and we would often go over to Martin Quinn's house, who was my brother Martin's grandfather, and eat a great meal. Martin Quinn would always be incredibly well dressed – dressed better than anyone. One of my favourite things about being a Traveller is the way we stick so close as family, it's just beautiful to me.

We would even bring country people in sometimes; I remember old Maggie Quale, who I used to get my clothes off when I was young, Paddy Quale and a chap called Bossy. Bossy would come over to our house and we would all just eat together, never any ceremony about it, we would get out the bread from the cupboard, the butter and jam from the larder and just eat while having a good natter, enjoying each other's company and the community spirit. Them days were just the best of times to be alive. I often think, if I could turn time back, I would love to live in those times again, the world just seemed so much more simpler. You never heard of any paedophiles or rapists and you certainly did not seem to see them in the media, on television and in the papers like today. It all seemed much slower and friendlier then.

I guess that's being young. Maybe we don't really live in the real world around us, it was just wonderful. Then I became an adult and it's like the box of chocolates opened up and started to melt. Everyone wants to bite a bit of you, you come above yourself, all for the wrong reasons. You find yourself in the fight and your name goes further than you can go. There are not many older Travellers around anymore, you know in their fifties and sixties and only God knows why that is. It's not because we die younger now, but because… well I don't really know!

These men though, were of my time, they were all doing well financially and this was some of the reason I did what I did and joined them. We had respect at that time too. We had names to look up to and names to maintain. All of those names were all well to do people. People used to look up to them, they always had great cars, clothing and trailers.

They were good men for working and earning a living. They

weren't just boxing day-in and day-out, they were out making a living, working hard, every day of the week. There was only one day a Traveller would never do any work in those days and that was the Sunday. No matter what came up, you never worked on a Sunday that was the way Travellers were when I was being brought up.

Travellers are incredibly proud people, you are what you are, and when I say it like that… let me put it this way, I am so proud of it, I have been a Traveller all my life, I've been fighting to be a Traveller all my life because I was discriminated against from the day I was born.

In the old days we used to have a saying: "Country people like gorgeous people," when we say this we meant ordinary English people and that also included ordinary English, Irish or Scottish people, Canadian, American English simply meant: you talk different, act different, your house is different, how you dress, how you walk, how you look at people, everything is different.

Well, you still get a lot of people trying to be Travellers, and it was so stupid to us back then how they looked. You're born being a Traveller or you're not. You can't really be made one or become one just because you fancy being one. That would be like me trying to be made into a Countryman. It can't be done. You are what you are; a leopard can never really change its spots, I guess.

There's a lot of younger Travellers taking their lives. It's so sad, when they have all their lives in front of them, and when you're gone, you're gone and what do you leave behind? Pain and hurt.

Honest to God, you know you're living, you're so proud to know what you are, I know people don't understand why I would be proud to be a Traveller, but I am.

The best bit about being a Traveller is... the freedom, when I walk into a place, no matter how posh it is, I know I am the cock, I am a free man, you walk in, you get eyes on you, I am who I am. I'm more free than any man, I can go anywhere and do anything within the bounds of my own moral compass. A Traveller can get a living. Put him in a desert and he'll get a living out of it. They know how to make money, no matter what they are doing, Travellers are gifted, they work hard, they have no limits. From the minute a Traveller is born he is taught and learns how to do that.

When a true Traveller denies his name though, that is just so disappointing and heart-breaking. I remember this, on my life, I was at a big football match, a charity football match, in London, all the East Enders actors were there, Shayne Ward and everyone, you know, this, that and the other, all big 'A' listers and Shayne Ward was there too. And I saw Shayne, and I'm allowed to say that Shayne is a Traveller, he has Traveller blood and heritage in him, comes from a Traveller family, he's a thoroughbred Traveller.

"Hey Shayne, Shayne...," I shouted over to him, and he looked at me, and I knew the 'look' – listen, I'm quick! I am fast! I am more than life, but I knew he was going to be a sausage... he looked at me with the shame in his eyes, I could see he was thinking, 'Oh, don't talk to me ...' he was ashamed. He was ashamed! A lot of Travellers nowadays seem to be ashamed of what they are, but I also know plenty of Travellers who are multi-millionaires, but they work in businesses and move in high circles, but they don't forget where they come from. They are proud of where they come from. Most Travellers now, you know like Shayne Ward are born, bred and raised on a council estate and then they forget where they come from. It is what it is, I still like him, I have a lot of time for him, but if he's happy with his life, he's happy with his life! You should never forget where you come from. But then again, his family forgot where they came from too, nothing wrong with them, they'll mix with you, but they prefer not to mix with you for no reason other than they don't want to talk about Travellers. They are hiding theirs and your race and they are trying to hide what they are, what you are! And, like I've said before, for me a leopard can never change his spots, you are what you are, be proud of it, one day you're going to die, one way or another, you know you're born to die and you should have no regrets, denying what you are.

I know other Travellers love their culture. If you were watching the funeral on TV after Prince Philip died, God bless and rest his soul, you'll see a man with a wagon, and his Rolls Royce, well he's a very, very good mate of mine, and he pulled up there with his wagon that has what we call a triangle with a black pot on it, and the women were there with him too. Well, that chap, he's a multi-millionaire, and yet he didn't forget, he went there with a wagon and a horse, and his Silver

Spirit Rolls Royce behind him, as a matter of fact it was a Phantom behind him, to pay his respects and showed all that you don't forget who you are.

Travellers don't travel all the time and travelling is dying away now, you can't really travel any more, all you can go to now is fairs, this new policy the government took out, anything over six trailers is a standing issue and they can take the things off you, you try doing that to another ethnic minority and it would be racist and cause all sorts of problems. If you're a Traveller you're treated as a nobody, you know? We are still under attack, massively discriminated against, just like other ethnic minorities, we are still fighting for our equal rights even in this day and age.

Travellers are all painted with the same brush and we shouldn't be. I don't care who it is, there's good and bad amongst everyone, all walks of life, and we're always painted in a bad way. If you ever see us on telly, anything you ever see paints us in a bad light: the Travellers are back or the gypsies are here – you only see bad news, you see them as dirty, dirty, shitty camps, you see all the gas bottles, they only show the rough part, they never show the cleanliness of the site, the media does that to us and how is that fair?

What people don't realise, and even though we don't travel that much anymore, they don't see how free and happy we are when we are travelling or on a journey, on the open road… following our ancestors. When I drive a wagon and a horse or a horse and trap, you get the wind hitting you in the face, you see the most beautiful sights, oh Mammy, Mammy, all you're doing is five to ten miles an hour with a wagon or twenty-five miles an hour with a horse and trap, it feels like you're in a Ferrari convertible. The wind is hitting you and honest to God, the world stops there. Everything's so lovely.

I remember me and my Roseanne, we went to Scunthorpe, we'd not long lost our Patrick and we were there, just there to be alone with our thoughts and memories. My father had given me a black mare as a present and I bought a nice sulky, a spinner, it was absolutely beautiful. So, me and Roseanne were going out on it every morning along the country roads and I got in with all the people in the village, and they would say,

"How are you, Mr Doherty?"

I'd salute them as we went past, returning their hellos and the scenery was so handsome, the atmosphere so relaxed and carefree, and I'm not ashamed to admit this, but we'd pull in at the side of the road in a lay-by and me and her would have a kiss and a cuddle. Money, no amount of money, if I won the lottery ten times over, no money could ever buy that moment, I'll tell you that! We'd have a little chat, another nice kiss and a cuddle and then we'd go on again. We'd take a shortcut through this farm, and the farmer would be like, "Hiya, Paddy, how are you?"

"Yeah, we're all right." I would reply.

Every Sunday morning, we'd go on the horse and cart, and it would feel like you were connecting back to your roots, never forgetting where you are and who you came from! Just beautiful. No matter who you are. You can dress me, you can clean me, you can polish me and yet the Traveller will always break out of me! Even if you're a Countryman and you join the Traveller way of life, sooner or later the Countryman will come out in you, it's bred into you, you can't deny it and you can't stop it happening. Your grandaddy and grandmammy will come out in you. No matter what you do, your breeding will come out in you. I could raise a Countryman from a brand-new baby, but yet the original breeding will come out in you eventually. It's a way of life, it's what you are, it's bred in you, it's in your blood, your DNA.

Country folk might believe in God, have a normal wedding or a christening or a baby shower for example. No Travellers really, would be into that, in that way, they're more into the '*Full Monty*' shall we say. Say for instance now, I've got a daughter who is going to be married; using my own daughter as an example; when she was getting married, I went to the man she was marrying and I said, "Listen I will give you a great do. I'll find a normal pub, food, everything and I'll put twenty-five thousand pounds in your account."
When you're paying for a wedding and you have the pub, you've just got to keep spending no matter how many people come along or were invited, it's your responsibility just to buy all the food, keep buying the rounds and looking after people no matter what and that's just part of being a Traveller parent.

The trouble is, now though, people are trying to outdo each other. So, if one family spend so much money on a wedding or funeral then the next family just want to spend more on theirs, just seems to be part of the way right now, so everybody is spending money on top of money and more besides, sometimes money they haven't got! Part of it is to show your wealth, to show off your welcome, to show who we are and what we are.

There are some really big names in the Traveller community and some extremely wealthy people. When people die, people seem to hire big cars, Bentleys, Rollers, huge fleets of cars and all I can say is you should go just as far as you can go without breaking the bank. It's more important to look after your family than it is to look good.

I find it really sad, not in the fighting way, but in what they think they have to spend (never mind what they are able to spend) to make themselves look better than the other. So, funerals have become sometimes a way of showing your wealth. If you come from a well to do Traveller family then you are having a five-star, wow factor funeral no matter what.

Christenings are starting to become the same. If you have the wealth you have to show it and it will often go on for a week or more. All Travellers are very different, but they are an intensely proud people.

Plus, if you have a big funeral, a big wedding, a big birthday party or a big christening, you're letting people know who you are and what you are and you're establishing your status, putting it down in the world for everyone to see.

No, I would say that is fantastic to do if you can afford it, really afford it, but a lot a Travellers are doing it now and they don't really have the money. I would say more luck to anyone if you can do it, do it, but if you can't please don't get yourself into debt to do it. Be what you really are and be happy. Travellers go out of the way sometimes to do it when they really shouldn't.

It's a bit like my father, your father pumps everything into your head; who you are and what you represent; Lord of the things my father taught me, was to never look down on anyone. He was a very well to do and a wealthy man. He used to say to me, "Be proud of who you are and what you are and carry your name with pride." That's all me and all my family learned to carry as it was passed on. That is how I learned to carry my name, it's the same with all my brothers and sisters and I have passed the same idea down to all my children, generation by generation of being proud to be yourself. You do have to carry yourself with a lot of dignity and a lot of pride, however, you get a lot of Travellers that have quite a lot of wealth now, new cars, top clothing, jewellery etc. yet sometimes, some of them look down on people.

Now anybody with wealth – good luck to them – but no one should look down on anyone else, it does not make you the better person just because you have the money.

To look down on someone because you are richer than them, to me, is incredibly disrespectful to them and to yourselves. It might seem a bit strange, but one of the things my father requested just before he died, was that his sons should not cry at his funeral. He wanted us to show and hold our respect and strength just the way he did.

To a lot of Travellers, wealth is everything. To me you either have it or you don't. To me, if you've got it, you've got it, if you haven't, don't worry about it, don't cry about it. Happiness is everything in the whole wide world, same with your health, it's not a lottery, but if you've got good health then you may as well be a lottery winner! Having your health and your strength are a lottery win in themselves. You could have millions of pounds but if you're dying of cancer, what use is it to you? There is no one rich in the grave!

Travellers are very proud people. I am very proud; I am more than proud of my wife. One of the things I really, really, love about Travellers is that they are an incredibly proud people. That shouldn't be confused with vanity, they are not vain people, they are just proud to be who and what they are and will defend their right to be so. To me it is a gift to be a Traveller and I am so very proud of my people.

It's like Country people, all gorgeous or whatever you want to call it, and the way they look at you, you can see exactly how they view you, what they think of you. That sort of, looking down their noses, haughty head lifts… you know what I mean. Not all of them, of course, but you can see they think you are the lowest of the low if you're a Traveller. Yes, if some of them want to come back to your home and you let them, you can see the surprise in their eyes because they didn't realise that you would have the latest, all singing, all dancing television, or that wonderful carpet, or that fantastic furniture, or that you could be dressing in such a fabulously well-dressed way. Stereotyping us. Well, it doesn't wash with me!

Travellers are incredibly proud people. The way they dress their girls is amazing and it's not just for special occasions, the girls take pride in their appearance and will be well-dressed and made up most of the time. Hell, we have sometimes been regarded as having a funny culture, we do get boys and girls marrying outside of our culture, but I always view it as I don't care who you are, what you are, you cannot pick and choose who your daughter or son falls in love with.

Now, I am sure you all know of Epsom Downs. Since we were children, we have been going to Epsom Downs; my father has always gone there and years and years ago he used to make trailers and roamers. He had a great name at the time amongst the Travellers. He used to deal in these and other things. As a matter of fact, he was known at the time, as James Bond, 007…

That's what his name was like, it was not gained at the fighting like others, he was known as 007 because he was respected as a true gentleman, and therefore, he had a true gentleman's name. I am going back now to when I was about seventeen years old. At that time, my old man had: two Rolls Royce's, four Jubilees, four Malcolm's, four Westmorland Stars, four Portmasters, Vickers, you name the trailers or caravans, he had them! Not bragging about this just an observation about my old father at that time. So, this is over forty-five years ago now and at that time he had over two hundred thousand pounds worth of tackle, a huge amount of money in those days, as you can imagine.

He was constantly dealing, bang, bang, bang, swap this, swap that, so fast, he was like lightening. That was what he was known for, dealing in all these trailers, 'The Blacksmith', the greatest dealing man in the world, well, he certainly was to me. He was at that time the 'Greatest Irish Dealer' on the planet! ON THE PLANET!

My father, not because he was my father, 'Black Simey Doherty', was simply the greatest dealer amongst Irish and English Travellers at that time. Everything would happen in Epsom, in the pub he used to go to, it was his office in so many ways. I used to love watching my old fella, how he would do it all, swap this car for that, an older trailer for another one and so on. He was dynamite at it when he was working, no one could touch him. All the time he would be winning, winning and making a profit no matter what. So clever at it. It would take your breath away to watch him work. Quite often he would do twenty to thirty deals in a day, always making money on the swaps and sales. So clever. He would finish off the day and he would often have a little drink or two, get a little drunk, but be happy with the trading of the day.

He often used to go to the 'Gambling School'. This was a big square, with scaffolding tube around it, and you would have three men allowed to go in, to what they would call the toss ring. One man would pick up the pennies, the other would take the bets and the other would toss the pennies up. I remember seeing my father losing one hundred thousand pounds in one day, just unbelievable. Of course, he won many a time, but not always.

I used to say to him, "Old man, what have you done?" When he lost big time in this way, he would say to me, "My Patrick, don't worry, they are borrowing that off me, I will get that back, don't worry. I will get a lot more than that back my son!"

He was just so confident about this and himself, not in an arrogant way but pure confidence.

He would never drink during the day when he was trading but only in the pub afterwards, always followed by the tossing of pennies for the craic.

Now I thought, and still do, that Epsom Downs was one of the best places in the world, Epsom Downs. I always loved the Appleby horse fair, of course, but to me it never compared to the Downs. Just a stunning place to be.

I remember we had the greatest time in the world. Epsom then was like, the 'Derby', the 'Grand National' all thrown in together. Everyone wanted to be there in the travelling world. You got thoroughbreds, every mixture of every breed, English, Welsh, Scots, Irish, every fucking breed. You just knew you could get it in there in any way you liked.

At that time there were a couple of brothers called Wally and Jimmy Stockings. Two good, solid English men. I remember young Wally was fighting a cousin of mine, it was only a small little ring and I remember jumping in and saying, "Hold on,

I'll fight," it was a good one!

Every morning we would wake up me and Johnny, we would get onto the racecourse and run the full lap of it. Every morning a full lap of it and it's a long way, we ran the whole thing, as fit as kings we were. This was like a Christmas present to the both of us every day.

Now it has changed so much and Travellers have changed along with it. I go there now because me and my brothers made a promise to our father. Before he died, he said, "Whatever happens," he told us, "every year go to Epsom, go to Derby Day." We promised him we would, so that's why we still go. To us Derby Day was the main day at Epsom, not because of the races, it was the main day for all Travellers.

As I said before, my father was a rich man, but Epsom put him a lot richer and his name 'James Bond, 007' spread like wildfire. My old fella would do a deal with someone and say, "You're okay, take the trailer," this was without a penny crossing hands on that day. He would take it on trust that they would pay him and of course they always did. He had a way of sussing people out and knowing if they were good for their word. I think if it was the right deal, my father would swap the suit off his back.

Every morning his dealing would start around nine o'clock, he would be up without fail at six-thirty to seven o'clock, have a wash and shave, in a bowl of water, in the open air. It was a great sight to see him outside with a basin of clean water. To me, I always remember my father as being an outstanding, good-looking man, his hair was coal black and he was a fine body of a man.

He would then go to see if his horses were fine, he always had good horses and great greyhounds with him. He loved them and their spirit. He also had good little Jack Russell Terriers.

Epsom Downs on Derby Day is the day we celebrate his life, no matter where I am or what I am at, I have to get on a plane or drive to that place, at that time, to be with him, celebrate him, along with my brothers Johnny, Kieran, Barny, Tony, Simey, we all have a beer for our dad.

Our Francie, God rest his lovely soul, we think of him and

celebrate him too.

I remember whenever we mentioned Epsom to my old fella, his eyes would light up with glee. When he became that age, eighty-one I think, it was like he would just light up and become young again on its mere mention, the memories rising and filling his mind with joy.

At age eighty-one he respected everyone but did not give a damn what they felt or thought. He knew the world and he knew people and any man he praised, which was so very rare, you knew then that that man was a good man true.

When I think of Epsom I think of my dad and I also now think of my nephew Michael Connors, my sister Mary's son. He got buried at Epsom and that was his wishes. Also buried there is my nephew's son, Tom. My brother-in-law Tom's boy and all his family's buried there. Epsom holds so many memories of people gone but never forgotten. So, when we go, we celebrate all of them, our history living in our hearts.

Now if I live to be a hundred, I don't want to live that long! I would like to live to eighty and then die. Epsom Downs will always be a part of me, it won't be part of my children because they don't know, it's a different environment and place now with different memories for them.

You see some great men at Epsom Downs. I have seen many a man going in with the best turn outs that a man could wear. A cousin of mine also called Paddy Doherty – 'The Guinness' he was called, his nickname because he always loved the Guinness. I remember him going in one day with a brand-new, pristine, white Range Rover. Going back years ago when they were special and they only made them with two doors, also a brand-new Malcolm trailer, and a brand-new Transit van, the best of the best!

I remember him walking out with his hands in his pockets saying to his women,
"Come on we have lost everything!"
He gambled and lost it all, lock stock and barrel – the Range Rover, the trailer and the brand-new Transit – all were gone just like that.

I remember my father giving him a motor to put all his stuff into. That's how gambling was in them days. It's the way it was and your name went before you. Every time me and my brothers go there, we go and get to one pub in the Downs and we get one pint for my father, God rest his soul, and of course the 'Old Queen', his lovely woman.

Great memories! Epsom Downs will always be great memories for me. Always a great part of my life. All the other meets and fairs don't. While they have a place, they do not hold my heart like Epsom. Just amazing memories that will live well with me until the day I die.

Another place I used to love was Doncaster. We used to have a regular meeting there and of course, we also went to Newcastle for a lot of meetings, yes, we had a regular fair there too.

It's great to be living in the same era as Tyson Fury and Billy Saunders and to be able to see what they do for other people in life, while helping people to understand that Travellers, like most people are good people, it's fantastic, just fantastic.

It's good that Travellers are being recognised these days. Tyson Fury, Billy Saunders, Tommy Ward who is coming up, young Cash, all these are travelling people and it's great to see that in the last ten years since I did *Celebrity Big Brother*, these people are finding their right place in the world. It's so much harder for Travellers, they often tried but did not fit into the world the way it is all organised.

I am so very proud of what they and I have achieved mainly because everyone looks at Travellers in a bad way, but the tide is hopefully turning and most people look at Travellers in a different way now.

## _Fighting_

If it wasn't a part of the Traveller lifestyle, I would say that this could be where it all started for me – at school. Bullying…

It's a funny old world when you look at it… Is it rags to riches or the other way around?

For me, it has gone both ways. When I was a young fella, maybe about eight years old, I had to go to school. Now I absolutely hated school, I hated it that much it was like the devil hates holy water.

It wasn't just the bullying or the fact that I was a Traveller and struggled with my learning, or that the teachers didn't like me, it was the shameful fact that I had to go to school with no knees in my trousers, holey shoes, too big for my feet and falling off, odd or no socks at all and off-coloured shirts with buttons missing. The other kids would make a laughingstock out of me then of course; I just used to get so embarrassed to be there.

It's not that I cared what they called me, I didn't care, it had become a way of life for me to be called dirty, smelly, scruffy, thick gypsy and all that. I found that I had come to terms with all of that, it just became a way of life and somehow you knew it and just sort of accepted it. Travellers learn through time to live with being slagged off.

When I was young, there was a rag-n-bone man, a really good rag-n-bone man, there were lots of them around in that time. This chap was a great judge of everything, and he would get really great clothes and other things. He found really nice tops, jeans, jumpers, trousers and great shirts, not designer labels, but they were real quality clothes. No odd socks, just proper pairs of socks with no holes in them. I remember we often found ourselves with odd socks in those days but you wouldn't care as long as they didn't have holes in them and they were clean. There was a woman called Maggie Quale, I will never forget her, God rest that beautiful soul. She was a very clever woman; she would get the clothing off the rag-n-bone man, she would wash and iron them, get them looking brand new and then she would sell them. I remember hanging around with her two sons, Paddy and Tony, lovely two boys who are still alive today. She had an idea how poor we were with my mum on her own and she would say, "Come in here Paddy and put these on ya."

Just wonderful! Clean, stunning, beautiful clothes. She really liked me I guess and cared for me. Her husband was called Paddy, so it might have been the name that did it? Ha-ha! I used to put these clothes on and I would say to the lads, "Oh, I do look good!" It felt great, the bees' knees at last.

No one ever knew I had got them off a rag-n-bone man but I certainly wasn't ashamed – I looked good and I felt good. I guess from that experience, I learned that it's not what you wear, but it's how you look and how you present yourself that makes the difference, you don't need designer names to look, feel and act good. I still love wearing good clothing to this day.

Eventually I grew to like school after moving to a new one called St Francis, I loved it! You had to wear a uniform and my mother was lucky enough to get a school grant. A brown blazer, a brown and gold tie with a pair of brown pleated trousers and brown shoes. Stunning new clothing, brand new, not second-hand or third-hand or well-laundered, BRAND-NEW CLOTHING! I could not believe it. I have to say, I felt so good in that uniform, I thought I was the gift! I remember taking huge pride in my tie, making it neat and pristine along with all of my clothing. It was just lovely to be as good as everyone else.

I remember feeling like life was beginning to get better for me. I was happy, I was proud to wear my new clothes, the other kids seemed to ease off my back a bit, things couldn't get any better as far as I was concerned. Just my luck though, it all changed when I went to high school. Unfortunately, here was where it started to go downhill again. I used to get a beating off some thug or other nearly every day. It wasn't all bad though, I will never forget I got in a with a chap called Phillip Boswell and after the initial sizing each other up and the odd scuffle here and there, we became very good friends and we still are good friends now.

At school Philip Boswell was the gamest of men, the guts he had were just unbelievable. He was a proper dare devil; he didn't seem to care how high a roof was, he would jump off it and he'd climb up guttering pipes so high you just could not believe it, just like spiderman on steroids was Philip. We became really close pals, like brothers in many ways, at that time he was my best mate and I thought I would never have a truer friend like him.

Him and another lad called Francie Wright used to mind me when I had trouble with other lads at school and outside of school. It was like having my own private bodyguards, Francie was a big lad!

I started to look after myself when I learned how to box and one particular lad used to pick on me constantly, he was a prefect, I remember, a really big bully of a lad. He used to stand on the staircase with his lackies at school and one day I was heading past him, minding my own business and I just knew he was going to have a go at me like he always did. He gave me a big push, nearly knocking me down the stairs but I turned round and gave him one almighty belt. Wham! He started to fall down the stairs and as he was rolling down the steps I was running after him to give him some more of his own punishment at last. I got on top of him and started to give him a few blows, then two other prefects pulled me off and I heard myself saying, "Your dead, your dead, I am going to beat ya!"

I'd had enough over the years of being bullied and finally found a way out of it. Suddenly all the other boys wanted to know me and knock around with me, I had found a key to my strength at last.

In the end, me and the prefect became good friends. He said to me one day, "I didn't realise I was doing that to you, you know, it just sort of happened automatic like."
I said listen, "Every time I was coming past you, you were giving me a crack and pushing me for nothing!"
He told me he was sorry and we became good friends. I have never held a grudge to anyone who does that, even to this day now, I will not hold a grudge if someone says sorry and means it. I will give them a hug and a kiss and all is forgotten, then move on.

If I do wrong, I like to think that I am man enough to say I am sorry too, it takes a man to own the bad things that he does. If we do wrong, we should apologise and say sorry, it's a small word but it has a very big meaning when it's meant true.

Eventually I went to a school called St John Vianney, this school was for people with special needs. Most of the other schools I had been to, had neglected me when I was really young and I spent a lot of time at the back of the class or in corners. I had been neglected in so many ways and eventually they found out that I was severely dyslexic. This school was to help me catch up with reading, writing and spelling and in a way to think faster and keep to the same pace as other kids my age.

I had a massive argument with a black kid, I think he was called Cedric, can't remember what it was all about now but he said to me, "I am going to stab you."
I remember him running at me with a garden fork. I am smiling, thinking of it now, he chased me around for what felt like hours, to within an inch of my life. I was fit as a fiddle and a good runner in those days, so he didn't get to me. Later that day I said to him, "I'm going to fix you."
It was a dog-eat-dog situation and I knew if I didn't sort him, he would have done me over.

At that time, we used to have these big coats called parkers, big, green coats with a big hood on them. I remember waiting for him in the playground, it was raining heavily and big dark clouds filled the sky, so it was cold, grey and miserable and not really where you wanted to be for a long period of time. He came out of school with the hood up on his parker and I remember saying to myself, 'I'll get him now!' He was a really big lad but with the boxing I'd been learning and practising, I had developed more confidence in myself.

I went straight up to him and without hesitation gave him an almighty crack in the face. Then I heard myself saying, "Your dead now." I swiftly pulled his hood down over his face so he could not get his head up and I punched his face and kept punching, swift and hard, then the head teacher arrived, Mr Clancy his name, well he eventually dragged us apart.

"What happened?" he asked.

"He ran at me with a pitchfork, threatening to kill me," I said.

The head teacher asked Cedric, "Did you?"

Cedric denied it saying, "I did not," blood dripping from his nose.

"You did!" I said, "that's why I got you like this, to defend myself."

"I really will kill you next time." Cedric said.

Well, that was like pouring fuel on the fire, I let him have it again, full throttle, breaking his face apart, even as the head teacher watched on.

"You going to kill me now?" I heard myself shouting as I pummelled his face again.

"No man, NO MAN, NOOOOOOO MAN, I WON'T I PROMISE!!" He screamed through his bloody mouth and face.

So, I stopped. I swear on my life, we became real good friends after that and I used to regularly go around to him and his Mummy's house when they lived in Moss Side.

She would do us a fantastic dinner. He was the only son and, in the end, I just loved so much to go around to his house for a big dinner and friendship. His mother was a lovely, kind woman. I was lucky in so many ways making friends like him, with families who were able to care. A lovely, lovely woman she was and a very caring and compassionate person not to be forgotten. So that was my time at school, I hated it when I was small but the last two schools were good.

I was never a bully. I never fought anyone who didn't need to be fought, but that is the past. Now at one time I just loved to fight, it was my life, it was *the* game. My name would go before me. Now to me one of the greatest travelling men in the country was Dan Rooney, then there was Paddy Cash, Michael Cash, Faila Rooney, my brother Martin, Joe Joyce, Snee Carlisle, our Dudlow – he was a hard, dirty fighter mind – he could fight just for fun and that's why he was called *'Rough Dudlow Ward'*.

He was one of those men who took no mercy on you, if you fought him, you had to fight his way and you knew by the end of it you would be taking a trip to hospital. He was called *'Rough Dudlow Ward'* and when they called him that believe me, they never named him wrong. He was my brother and I loved him; I loved our Dudlow so much. I can remember when he got very sick, I got a private hairdresser to go to the hospital so he could have a haircut, just to lift his spirits a bit – I just loved him, God rest his beautiful soul and his lovely wife Meggie who was known as Dudlow's Meggie, never just Meggie, always Dudlow's Meggie.

One of the best fighters was called Ned Rooney who was a fine fighting man, he was one to fight all right if you had the chance, he could fight for fun shall we say. I remember we fought three times and he never gave best to me and of course, I never gave best to him. Giving best is when you give way and say that the other fighter has won, with fighters like me and him we would never give way and we would carry on going to the bitter end when you just could not fight anymore. We fought for so long, every time we met, that we hurt each other badly. Even though we fought like we wanted to kill each other, we are now the best of friends. I have a lot of respect for Ned and vice versa, he has respect for me too.

There are other Rooney's: John Rooney, Felix Rooney and Larry Rooney all of them were nice chaps and always good for a fine fight, respect!

Some of the other fair fighters at the time were Johnny Coyle, my uncle Patrick another fella called Johnny Tuppence who was from Belfast. There were lots of great fighters at the time and they all had a name of sorts. I remember Nick Kiely who was the man to beat from Manchester at one point. All of them were great men and good men to fight, men you would look up to in the fighting game.

I guess you could say I was bred to be a fighter, it was in my blood, like a calling from the past that had to be followed, whether I liked it or not.

I will never forget Johnny Coyle and his brother Tony, both outstanding in their day, not forgetting Francie Coyle as well. Johnny was a southpaw and there were not many who fought like that in those days, my he could fight all right, and he made it all look like fun. I remember one chap called Bimbo Ward, a wonderful professional who was outstanding, in and out of the ring.

I remember years ago, some of the fighters of the time, Dan Rooney, Michael Cash, Andy Cash, Felix Rooney, Larry Rooney, Ned Rooney and of course the famous Joe Joyce. He had a nickname of 'The Hulk' for obvious reasons, he was built just like him and he did not give a damn for no one. When it came to a fight, he would not care who they were or what they were he would fight them.

Old Joe Joyce, never any backing, no big armies behind him, always just himself, he did not care who you were or what you were, old Joe Joyce was as good a man has ever thrown a coat off. He was an outstandingly, great man. My father thought so and he was a good man in my day too. He has a son called Joe. Joe is as good as his father was, it is bred in him. To me, outside of Tyson Fury, in the ring, he is the greatest boxer in the world.

Out on a street fight then, young Joe Joyce is an outstanding champion of a man and this can never be taken away from him. This man cannot refuse anything. The minute anyone throws down a challenge to him, he takes it up, he just cannot say no. It does not matter who they are or what they are, whatever their weight – it is irrelevant to him. He is so superb about training and being an athlete to himself, he is super fit and goes total super fit when training and will fight anyone no matter what. Better than that though, he is a total gentleman. I have always found him to be one of the best, just like his Daddy. But this young Joe Joyce is in his twenties and I would say he is the gamiest travelling man on the planet. He will fight you till he dies, he is so committed, but on top of all that he is a gentleman to go with it. With drink or without a drink, I have always found him a very nice man, I have never had anyone slag him off to me at all, ever. All Joe will ever want is a good craic, a proper gent, his brother is the same and his older brother John now gone, God rest him.

Many of my family were in the game, my uncle Francie Doherty, uncle Johnny Doherty, uncle Barney, a great man, my old uncle Patrick, just an amazing fighter, Johnny Tuppence, Blondie Simey, all great men, great at the game as indeed, all six of them were in the fighting scene.

Now my brother Martin was nothing to look at as a fighter but my, he could knock 'em dead with one punch; he had a punch like an elephant; it would be like they had been hit with an elephant's foot, unnatural the way he knocked 'em down, Bang! Wallop good night! My brother Martin was an amazing fighter, a legend in his own lifetime, in my opinion. When he was a young fighter, you could not believe the strength of the man. He was only about eleven stone in weight but he was one of the best street fighters, the most natural I have seen in my life. A great fighter, nothing to look at, so to speak, but my God could he fight. The truth is I used to envy him at how good he was, he was just fantastic and I am not saying that because he was my brother. Like lots of brothers, we have had thousands of fights of course, sometimes physical. He would beat me sometimes and other times I would beat him, there was never one better than the other.

People would say to me, "Who is the better man?" and I would say, "Oh, our Martin without a doubt," and they would ask him the same question and he would say, "Oh, that would be our Paddy without a doubt."

So, people would never know who the better fighter was of the two of us. I have to say, at that time it was great to see him fight, if someone stood you a challenge, he would fight them, straight up, the next day. No training for six weeks or so, like you would find today, if someone threw down a challenge, it was taken up on the next day. Another thing about that time was that you either won or lost and you did not get draws like today, so it was always a fight to the bitter, bloody end no matter what. No matter how much your face was cut to bits, facially disfigured, bloodied and broken you just kept on going until one of you won. All his fights were always fair with no dirty play, just plain, honest, honourable good fights. He had some name, he was a legend of a fighter and never lost at all, some man! I remember him fighting Felix Rooney, a huge giant of a man, and did our Martin give him a bad beating! Don't get me wrong, Felix is a nice man, a great fella too but when I say he beat him, it was not just that he won, he gave him a good game, but Felix never gave way. To beat someone proper, they have to '*give best*', that means giving in to the other fighter and Felix never did that. As I said, my brother Martin was only eleven stone, all skin and bone in many ways and Felix was a walking muscle of a man, a fine figure, well-constructed and well-built like a machine. In the end the fight was stopped as both men had fought so hard and not actually won. To me, I would have said that my brother Martin was the better man, but I am biased, and it has to be said, Felix was good too.

Of course, the one amongst all of them with the greatest influence was my father, the one who made me, so in many ways I was blessed with the history, my ancestors passed the skill down, almost like a warrior clan you could say.

I had a lot of fights like Martin and of course, like him sometimes at the end my face would be unrecognisable, but you just accepted it as part of the game.

In fighting names, in my past, the greatest names would be: Doherty, Rooney, Cash, Purses… speaking of the Purses –

Michael Purse was a humdinger of a man to fight, in my day, it was Dan Rooney. He was a legend who fought anyone, he was simply the best. He had such a great name and was never beaten, bred for fighting and now, believe it or not, he has become a pastor, and works with God. In the Rooney boxing yard there is your Dan Rooney, Felix Rooney and Ned Rooney was the next outstanding man to fight. In his day he was simply the bees' knees. They were of course, all brothers. I can't leave out another outstandingly great man, John Rooney, as part of the pack too.

Another boxing family was the Coyle yard – Johnny and Tony Coyle who were just brilliant when they fought.

Another famous family were the Cash's: Michael, Paddy, Johnny and Andy Cash. You never forgot great men like them, they are legendary to me and their name was stuck in your memory and everyone else's and they were always discussed when talking about great fighting families.

Another great fighter was Martin McDonough, his nickname was '*Kojak*'. Another humdinger of a fighter, who could fight just for fun. Another famous name of the time was Nick

Kylie, he was the man of the time and I mustn't forget the Wards, who were something else as fighters.

I used to go to all of the fairs all over the country, particularly when I was a much younger man. I remember one of the first times I went, I saw a man go into this makeshift boxing ring, where they offered a tenner (which was a lot of money in those days) to anyone who would take on and beat this fighter. So, I watched a few people try out and I have to say, they were taking a good beating. What a sight that was. Fists flying, the landing thwacks, blood and spittle spraying out as the opponents' heads snapped away. It was exhilarating to watch and really got the blood heating and the excitement from the crowd was electric.

So, one particular day two people, Tom Ward and David McDonough (who eventually became my brothers-in-law) came to me and said, "We've got this man who is mad to fight you, Paddy!"
So, I thought about it for a minute, they hadn't even told me who it was or why or anything, but I said, "Ah, go on then." I had no idea who I was stepping into the ring with. It filled me with raw excitement and I was psyched up and ready to

go. I got to the ringside and my eyes popped out of my head, I couldn't believe what or who I was looking at! I have to say, the man waiting there genuinely looked like a werewolf! From the waist upwards, he was covered in this thick body hair that went right up to his neck, it was just like horsehair. I said to myself, 'Mammy, Mammy, Mammy, what is THAT in front of me?' I could see this fella was a big, old bear of a man and probably had the temperament to go with it, but I was cocky and arrogant, I put the gloves on, well not real boxing gloves, more like sparring pads but proper poor quality, neither use nor ornament really! Of course, this is like forty-five years ago, a long, long time ago for me, when I was in my prime, young, fit, ready to go at anything and anyone, you know, just what you are like when you're in your twenties, at the peak of my game (or so I thought).

Even though inside you are scared shitless, you don't show that to the watching world, do you? You don't show them the real you, just who you want them to think you are. It's like a game of poker – put on your poker face – put on this mask of bravery (cockiness in my case) because in my mind that's the battle half won already. Show no fear, know you will win no matter what, play the game of poker, show them no

114

weakness, no clues as to what's really going on in your head. Believe me, in my head I was like, 'Oh SHIT!!!'

A double first cousin of mine, Martin Ward, was in my corner geeing me on and on my life, I am not ashamed to say this, I walked towards the middle of the ring where the referee and wolf-bear man are waiting and it's worth noting that, although there is a referee in there with us, it didn't really matter in these circumstances, in this kind of fight. They were just there for show and to watch you beating each other to a pulp, beating the brains out of each other and to call time. They didn't intervene, there's no bloody rules anyway, so what's the point? Anyhow, I walk up to them in the middle of the ring and I said to the hairy monster, "Listen my friend, it's only a spar, a bit of fun. Let's just make it that shall we?" He turned his stony face to me, leaned right into me and spat back, "Listen to me cunt, if you can put me down, then fucking put me down 'cause if I can put you down, then I'm putting you the fuck down, so down, that you won't be getting back up again, ever! You got me? Now let's get the fuck on with this."
I knew this had gone from being a bit of a laugh with my cousins, a bit of a fun sparring match to something else

115

entirely. I knew he was going to try and pummel me into the ground, to hurt me so much that I wouldn't be getting back up off my own steam, maybe not even in an ambulance, you get me? This guy was so arrogant, so confident he could beat anyone, that the stakes had just got really real now, this was going to be a fight for my life.

We went back to our corners to wait for the start bell to sound and he did something I'd never seen anyone else do before; he smeared a load of Vaseline all over his forehead and the tops of his eyebrows, then across each cheekbone. I had no idea why he'd done that, but I was getting impatient to start so I looked at him hard and said, "Let's do it!"
'*Ding-Ding*' went the bell.
Straight away the punches flew, not little jabs to test reach, big, massive, swinging lunges that landed and landed hard. SMACK! SMACK! THUD! THUD! Real hard hits from the pair of us. I have to say he could take a punch and it was a very heavy, good first round for the two of us, just as we'd both hoped it would be. Neither getting the better of the other. That first round was all I needed to get the measure of him and understand his strength.

I am back in my corner, and the corner man said, "Ya all right, Paddy?"

"Yeah!" I fired back, "No problem. I'm taking him out now in this next round. Let's go!"

'*Ding-Ding*' and we were off, punches of steel flying everywhere, as quick as a leopard and hard as a brick. SMACK! Now, when you are in roughing it with each other in this scenario, the referee was not interested. No breaking us apart, just Hell fire non-stop. Pretty much the only thing you could not do was bite each other. All I stood to win on this one was five pounds and the loser; well, he would get nothing. Not much for a good beating, I can tell you. You might as well be saying you are paying a man five pounds to beat the brains out of you! Not if you are kinky – it's a good thing to be into but I was like, '*Not tonight, Josephine!*' I'd had enough of this guy and this fight, so I gave him the most vicious CRACK! on the side of the face and he dropped stone-cold to the floor. As he was dropping, when I knew I had him, I gave him an upper cut to the jaw and one more for good luck on the side of the head, feeling his brain bounce off the side of my hand!

I couldn't believe it, on the count of eight he gets up! Unbelievable! I swear on my life, he copped me a punch that sent me flying backwards from one corner of the ring to the other. I was still standing but it was like you see in cartoons, you fly backwards, then spin on the spot like a pirouetting ballet dancer! I looked towards him and all I can see are ten (not one) big, hairy, angry monsters charging towards me with the most savage leer contorting his face!

I am thinking to myself, 'which one is the real him?' No idea where to throw the next punch, I went on the back-foot to buy myself some time. This was the first time I'd ever had to do this in a fight. I came around slowly then see him come back into single focus, just the one ugly head grimacing at me now, thank God. BANG! BANG! I let him have it: hard left and right, like fire breathing from a dragon. He made a swing at me, missed, and I fired a shot right into his kidney. He let go this almighty ROAR! Just like the wolf-bear I described him as, but this time like a trapped animal screeching for his Mummy. The minute I heard that, I knew I had him and WALLOP! I gave him another hard shot and just as he was about to fall down again… '*Ding-Ding-Ding*', the bell goes again. 'Argh, fuck that bell,' I thought to myself as I went back to my corner.

Third round and the beast is still standing, this guy is a machine, like bloody Dolph in the *Rocky* film, hit him hard, hit him harder, combinations, the lot. I'm thinking, 'Bollocks!' This guy is way better than I ever thought he was. He's still standing like a dishevelled statue! 'Oh, maybe he's a proper werewolf or werebear,' I think, then he runs straight at me again, across the ring like a big sausage. Just as he gets to me, I hit him with a left and a right at speed, his jaw cracked and he went to the ground with an almighty CRASH!

One… Two… Three… Four… "Stay down, you bastard," I shouted… five… six… seven… 'What the fuck?' I couldn't believe it – he starts to get up again! Mad eyes glaring out of his head, his face in a set grimace, staring over in my direction. He's pushing himself up off the floor, on all fours now but as soon as one of those hands left the floor, then I was straight in there, on him again, as the loose rules allowed. I was on him, my silver bullets ready to finally slay the beast. I let him have at least five quick blows, the hardest hits I've ever given, with the speed and force of cannon balls, I laid into him around his head, and he collapsed back to the floor.

He groaned and sighed as he sank into the floor, like an animal finally succumbing to its fate when caught in the mouth of a lion, almost a whimper, a dribble of saliva mixed with the blood from his battered face. The groaning stopped and the next thing I saw was paramedics rushing into the ring to sort him out.

I was announced the winner and awarded the measly five pounds prize money, alongside a good black eye, a pair of lips like *Mick Jagger* and bruises all over my body for five pounds, five fucking pounds! MAD! All the boys were saying to me, "You are some man to beat him, some man you are, Paddy Doherty!"
I sub-consciously rolled my eyes thinking, 'Yeah, some man you are, Paddy, more like a CLOWN!'

I went home to my woman who was just finishing drying up the dishes in the kitchen and she turned around and dropped the plate as she sees me, the dish smashing into a million bits on the tiled floor. She said, "Oh Paddy, what happened?"
I told her the story, how I fought this guy for five pounds and she looked me in the swollen eye, hands on hips and said,

"Ya dirty idiot you! For five pounds you went and fought a man for that and he did that to you, you must be out of your tiny mind!"

I told her how Tom and my brother-in-law had gotten me into it and that I couldn't really say no because I had a name to defend. At the time, I had a name like a racehorse, so I was not going to let myself get slagged off. Well, I did it, I beat him and God was good to me, as I did it with class.

As a young man, even with this mad fight, I got to love the fairs, the Traveller fairs are just a great part of our culture. My cousin Johnny Coyle, who was with me, said, "Fair play to you Patrick, fair play to you. You done it in style."

I remember going to the pub the night of the fight and there was big gambling going on upstairs, like a one hundred pounds stake on a game of pool. So, Johnny played a fella for a hundred pounds and beat him and the man demanded another game double or quits. So, Johnny played him again and won him fair and square. He again insisted on double or quits and by this time now owed Johnny four hundred pounds. So, I said to him, "Look, pay him the money you owe him, give it up as a bad job, I'm having a game now."

He turned to me and said, "Listen to me 'monkey'…" Like in the saying, *'I'm talking to the organ grinder not the monkey.'*
Well, no one gets away with that, I am no one's monkey and you can't put me down using that. So, I cracked him one! No good in giving him a hug and saying, "What did you say?" He knew very well what he was up to. BANG! BANG! He dropped to the floor. Immediately there were four more onto me. Johnny Coyle my cousin ran over and both of us smashed up the four of them before they could get a punch in at us. They didn't know what had hit them but they lay whimpering on the floor with broken teeth and faces. We smashed these men up like there was no tomorrow, they looked like they had been through a grinder by the end of the fight. After that in those days, no one would tackle us, as we had a reputation and a name, when you have that, you have respect and the wrong ones leave you alone for the right reasons.

We were outside the pub, celebrating and laughing as young fellas do, and told each other how one had saved the other, laughed all the way to our home we did. We were woken up by a friend who'd had a call from another friend and he said to me, "Paddy – there's a mob on the way. After the fight in the pub last night, they are all coming down en masse to give it to you!"

I remember a guy called Harry (dead now) who we used to call '*Dirty Harry*'. We called him that because he would deal with anything, robbed motors anything, you name it, he did it. He was a lovely man, and so is his son who is in jail now, a lovely man. Two of the loveliest men in the world. So, Harry had warned us they were coming to get us, to beat us up after the fight in the pub. In those days I had a brand-new, white Volvo estate, and Johnny had a brand-new car too. Now under normal circumstances if you had a warning like that you would leave, but we couldn't do that because our name was going before us and we had to maintain that and maintain our respect in the community. Johnny Coyle and Paddy Doherty were big names in the Traveller community in those days and we had to maintain them. It wasn't just about us; it was a matter of pride for our family and our ancestors, that's simply how it all works.

Hundreds of men turned up that morning looking for us and I remember Johnny turning to me and saying, "Argh, we are bolloxed!" his face resigned with the recognition of impending doom.

So, Harry said to me, "Here's a gift," handing me a pump action shotgun.

Then I turned to Johnny and said, "Well, we got it now, one way or the other, we have it covered!"

So, we went out to face them all and one of the men shouts out, "Where's this little Paddy Doherty then?"

This really got my back up. In those days, I hated that sort of saying. I was a bit sensitive about my height because I was and still am, on the short side!

"Listen here," I said, "I'm right here, I am Paddy Doherty." We knew we were likely to get a real good beating here, so I said, "Listen here, who is the best man amongst you, the hardest, toughest one?"

This fella jumps out of the crowd of hundreds, "I am!" He said with a cocky grin all over his face, looking down on us, sneering, chest puffed out like a gorilla.

"Well, that's fair enough," I said, "what about me and you fight and leave everything and everyone else out of it?"

"Okay," he said.

"So, do I have your word that's the end of it? Once the fight is done, win or lose, it is done, we are all clear?" I asked.

Again, he says, "Okay."

So, me and the man we went out into the middle of everyone and I hit him – hard – Bing! Bang! Bing! He went down pretty sharpish, hitting the ground with a crack of the head. I hit the man clean and fair. So, I said to him quietly, "You're better off calling it a day, okay?"

But no, he turns round and again and starts saying, "Listen, little man…,"

"Look," I said, "we agreed up front, win or lose, it's done. I've done you right, I'm saying your right because I knew that with all these hundreds you brought that we weren't going to get out alive!"

I gave him a hand up from the ground and he knocked me down. The crowd by now are all shouting, "Good fight! Good fight!"

"Let's call it a day," I said.

We shook hands – no winner – no loser, all was well. No draw, no nothing the fight ended.

"I'll tell you what," he said, "for two young men on your own, you are game men, fair play to you."

Johnny said, "You are what you are. This was all blown out of proportion. We were playing ya man a fair game of pool, I bet him, he kept going double or quits and I kept beating him and plain and simple he did not want to honour the bet and pay up."

In the end, the fella said to us, "I can see that you are straight forward and honest men, the two of you."

Then we all shook hands and finally went back to bed again. I remember after that we left and went straight to Epsom Downs, me and my cousin Johnny.

I'm no longer into fighting thank God, for a man of my age it would be an embarrassment for me and my children, it wouldn't look smart, me getting into my boxing shorts now! I remember Tyson Fury and John Fury his father, the Fury's are outstandingly good men, in and out of the ring. Your name is everything, no matter what. Your father's name should be the greatest name on the planet.

I am what I am and I'd never back down from a man. Even though I would never back down or pull on the handbrake (as it's referred to in my world) nor would I have said any man is better than me or he is the best, but I would show respect to my elders or people I hold in high regard. This seems to be a bit of a generation thing, in my time you showed respect to your elders and women and that all seems to have gone out of the window nowadays.

A young chap would kill an old man now, in my day, you would never give anyone older than yourself any cheek.

## _Tight Spots_

When you're in a tight spot how do you think your way out of it? You see, I don't consciously think my way out of it, I know there is no way out of it, I just go with it. But as I'm going with it, I weed myself out of it, it's like you're in a deep hole and you've no way of getting out, you're in trouble, you can climb that hole and try to get out, know you've got to climb out of that hole, but as you're climbing you get more and more… stuck or slipping back down into the hole.

I've been cornered a million times that way and I end up coming out – beautiful. So, listen to this one, I was in a pub one day, with my brother Martin, the pub was packed, this lad came over, he said, "Err, you Paddy Doherty?"
I said, "Yeah."
"I'm fighting you!" He said.
"You're fighting me for what?" I asked.
"Because you're this, that and the other, you're the king of the Travellers, aren't you?" He said.
I won't say the actual things he said, but you can imagine!
"I'm no king…," I started to say but he cut me off.

"You fucking are, get outside, come on let's go…," he insisted.

We went outside like he insisted and honest to God, there must have been about two hundred Countrymen all milling around, so I knew then what was going on. He had no intention of fighting me and I'm thinking, 'Oh, Shit! … this is a stitch up! I'm dead!'

"We're done Paddy, we're done for!" Our Martin said.

"No, watch this man…," I said.

I knew it, I knew I was in a corner, I knew beating this chap was no good, because then I'm getting a beating from all those Countrymen, and our Martin is going to get a beating too.

"Listen to me very carefully, before me and you fight, who is the best one here. Who is the best man out of all of you?" I asked.

I'm not kidding you, there were a hundred and fifty to two hundred Countrymen there, it felt like there were thousands. I knew I had to do something, because this was one fight I wasn't walking away from unscathed, even if I beat him.

"I'm the man here! Not him, me!" Another man said, who had pushed his way out of the crowd trying to look all menacing and to a rip-roaring chorus of cheers from the rest of the men.

"Well, I'll fight you then. I'll beat you then!" I said to the man.

He looked me up and down, turning back to face the crowd all cocky, chest puffed out, smarmy grin all over his face, arm pointing towards me, and as he turns back to answer me, he raises his voice so everyone can hear, "If you can beat me, you can walk. You can walk if you can beat me. But if I beat you, what do I get?"

"I'll leave, first thing tomorrow morning, we're gone. Okay? So, I'll fight you now, let's get on with it! And remember, you've given your word, I can walk out of here whatever the result!" I said back to him.

"Yes, I've given my word, you've got my word that you can walk out of here. You and your mate," he said.

"He's not my mate, he's my brother," I replied.

I love our Martin, he's my life, all my brothers are but our Martin's like my twin.

This calmness came over me completely. I kept myself soft voiced, stood in a non-threatening stance, completely relaxed on the outside but I have to be honest, on the inside it was a different matter though. The problem with having a reputation for fighting, is that everyone who thinks they are a hard man wants to have a go, but what they don't realise is that this is just who I am, it's not personal, it's a job to me. So, I knew I was getting a beating, par for the course in this job, I knew I was getting a beating by the head man and I had to take the opportunity to protect our Martin at the same time.

"Before we get started," I said to the man, "before we get started, you give me your word that I can walk out of here, with my brother, when this is all done."

"Listen, Doherty," he said, "I'm the governor here, what I say goes, now let's get it going."

We fought for a couple of minutes if that, dink, dink, pop, dink, done! He naps! He got one punch in; I didn't even feel it. He had no idea what he was dealing with. I'm so used to this now, that I don't even feel most of the hits anymore. I know it sounds crazy, but it's true. But obviously I knew that if I'd have taken on the other fool, win or lose (well win really) I knew me and Martin weren't walking out of there without a severe beating from the crowd!

A lot of people think I'm a mindless thug, but they are wrong, so wrong. I will walk away from a fight if I can, I'm not a young man anymore, I'm not afraid, never afraid, just weary of it all now, I don't have anything to prove to anyone. But I knew in this case I had to use my brain as well as my brawn. If I defeated the captain, if I beat the captain of the ship, everyone would disembark, you know like a mutiny! Dink, dink, dink... fuckoff!

To cut a long story short, me and my brother walked out, heads held high, no issues. And that's what you do when you're in a tight corner, brains first! When you realise you're in that corner, you've got to think carefully to find a way out, and that's what I did. It was a good move, because I knew otherwise, we were going to get a bad beating.

Here's a tale about another tight spot I found myself in, just because I am who I am. It can be very frustrating at times but I guess it comes with the territory, it comes with being a Traveller, it comes from being known and having a reputation.

I was in a pub in North Wales one New Year's Eve.

Everyone was merry and celebrating as you would expect and I was enjoying the moment myself when suddenly this young girl comes over to me. She's smiling and so on and suddenly she said, "You just pinched my backside!"

"Excuse me?" I asked in a bit of a shock.

"Let's put it this way, you just pinched my arse," she fired back with a sneer on her face.

"Excuse me, my darling, I did no such thing," I said, trying to edge away from her.

"You did!" She screamed at me.

I kept denying it and she kept on raising the temperature starting to draw attention to herself and of course me.

"Give me a hundred pounds and I will forget it and go away," she said to me with a crafty smile, the little minx!

"Not on my life," I said to her, getting really fed up with the girl, "I am giving you nothing, not a bean – No I am getting the police instead! That will clear this up nicely I think, don't you?" I asked her.

She dashed over to her mother who was nearby and I could see her saying all sorts of things as she pointed toward me with a finger. Of course, the next thing the mother comes across and starts accusing me of molesting her daughter.

"I did nothing," I said and told them to fetch the police.

Well eventually the police came and an officer is speaking to me.

"We have had an allegation that you assaulted that young lady over there Sir," he said.

"Officer, look," I said, "This place has cameras everywhere, take a look at them and rewind the video back to the time she said I did this and you will see it's all a load of made-up nonsense!"

"Okay," he said.

Fifteen minutes later and the officer is back. He beckons the girl and her mother over to where I was standing, the noise in the pub suddenly dies down in the anticipation that I'm about to be dragged off in cuffs by the law.

"You understand that you made a serious allegation about Mr Doherty, don't you?" The officer asked the young girl.

"He wasn't anywhere near you at all, until you went over to him. Do you still maintain that Mr Doherty assaulted you?" Suddenly she started to squirm, "I... I... didn't see who did it," she said, "it wasn't him. I am so, so sorry," she said, looking up at me with a sad, puppy face.

That didn't work on me like it would her mum or the officer and I wasn't letting her off the hook that easily. She needed to understand the consequences of her actions.

"You're sorry?" I said in a raised voice, "how dare you say that! How dare you accuse me of assaulting you like that? I have a gorgeous wife and I love her! I would never even dream of touching the likes of you!"

She squirmed and shrank away, the way she should. I hope she learned a lesson from that encounter, but I doubt it very much.

Later that night when I got home, I said to Roseanne, "You are not going to believe this – I was accused of pinching a young girl's backside tonight in the pub and the cheeky little sausage wanted a hundred pounds to 'make it go away'! Can you believe it?"

Roseanne looked at me with her mouth open in shock 'O'.

"Anyway, I think she… well I hope she learned a lesson because I made her fetch the police!"

"Did the police come, Paddy?" Roseanne asked me, "what happened then?"

"Yes, they came and I told them to look at the CCTV. They did and it proved I had not done anything wrong. The little minx was just trying her luck."

"Oh my!" Rosanne said.

To me this girl was only a child, maybe eighteen or so, a little baby to me. Why would I want a *Happy Meal* when I have a *T-Bone Steak* at home?

Roseanne is a gorgeous woman and I love her with all my heart. I am not something or someone to be played with by the likes of this little girl. My Roseanne is to me, the film star of all film stars, an absolute beauty queen to me.

This is one of the problems that can happen to you with my sort of fame. Some people are always happy to accuse you of things, try to fight with you or even ban you from a pub to get one over you. It saddens me sometimes that life is like that but I have to remind myself that most people are good.

It's a hugely shameful thing when you have people like this, trying to take advantage of you. They are often half my age or younger and look at me as a young man, someone who they would get known for if they won me in a fight. I am an old lion and I want nothing of this sort of thing anymore, my fighting days are done, end of story. All I want now is peace in life.

These days I am more careful who I mix with, as I get older, I take more care so as not to be in situations where people like this can try and take advantage. I do not want this type of thing around me, I am an aging man, a great, great, granddaddy, would you believe?

## _Family Life_

My father and mother had me before they were married, they were living together one would say. Eventually, they split up and both my father and mother got remarried.

Now my father got married to Lizzy Doyle who I called my 'Old Queen', and my mother got married to old Davey Quinn, I called him 'Old Quinn'. They always loved me, my Old Quinn loved me very much as he did my stepbrothers and sisters. He loved me like one of his own, God bless him, he truly adored me. I was so lucky, I must say, and of course my Old Queen adored me too. To think I was lucky enough to be gifted like that, with all that love, what a gift.

My mother is a fine woman, when I look at her now in her early eighties, she seems so very fragile, when she was a younger woman she was stronger than an ox, she was not afraid of anyone when she was young, if needed, she would take on the worst of the worst, she was bold and wouldn't let anyone talk over her if they were wrong. It's difficult to see her go from such a big brazen woman to a small delicate being. I love to go to see her two or three times a week now.

I go with my brothers and I go see her on my own as much as I can. I just love to see her on my own, as I then have her all to myself.

She will say to me, "Let me make you a cuppa tea my Paddy." "No Mummy, let me make it." Then I bring her a cuppa and we sit down and have the loveliest chat in the whole wide world.

We often have a good old talk about the past, what life was about. She loves to talk about her father and mother and her own past and it's a real joy to hear all these old souls coming to life through her words. We talk away and we don't hide anything, we have a laugh and a giggle and even if she says something wrong and I know it's wrong I say, "Your right, your right Mammy."

My great granny used to smoke a pipe and we have a good laugh about that now, in a kind way. Chatting with my mother is the loveliest thing in the world. As I always say, "Your Mummy is your Mummy and respect your mother now because you won't have her forever!" The time we have together is so precious, we think that the end will never come but of course it will come and this is one of my biggest fears in life. I just so dread the day I lose my mother and I just hope it's not for a long time yet. You only have one mother, always remember that and don't be afraid to show her love, give her love there and then, no matter what she has done or not done to you. When she is gone, she is gone forever and you are never going to meet her on this Earth or talk to her again. You should treasure your mother forever.

My mother has a big, lovely family, six girls and four boys. At her birthday celebration just recently, there was no one there only me, my brothers Martin and Dudlow.

I don't want to be like that – to live to that point in your life when you have so few people there. Eighty-one years of age, and no one is there for her. We can send messages, phone everyday saying, "Oh, I love you, Mummy – how I would like to be there, but sorry, I can't be there with you. I hope you have a great day." Then you send flowers and all that type of shite! GET YOURSELF THERE! Eighty-one years of age! When your family members get past seventy-five, we know it's limited time we have left with them. We should make an effort to be with them. It's only ONE DAY! What is one day out of our lives, to give them the happiness and the memories and appreciation of their love?

I am sick of the games, from the young ones today, all the crocodile tears, "I love my nanny!" None of my sons will ever go to see their grandma, my daughter yes, but my sons and their children, no! It's too late when they are gone!

My daughter, Margaret, truly loves my mother, I think partly because she knows how much I adore my mother and love her. I also adore my wife!

My brothers are exactly the same.

My father is gone and I miss him so much, I miss my old man so much, the pain is unbelievable sometimes. I find myself thinking about him as regular as clockwork. I think to myself, 'He is the man who made me the man I am now, be it good or bad, he made me the man I am now.' That is why we should love all people as you would yourself.

Now my father was a rich man! I remember going to the tailors with him, and he would get all his suits made by hand. For Epsom, for the Downs, always going to the same tailors all the time. I go to the very same tailor myself now and have been doing for years, long before my father ever died. Superb fitting, fine cloths that make you feel great, the bees' knees! I am very lucky to know them. I wear the same style as my father, a very special cut and pattern that is instantly identified with us. Some would say it's old-fashioned but it is nice, I feel it's lovely and I look great, in the way they cut them for me.

When I put on my suit and shoes, I feel as if I have my old fella with me! I know you might think that a little crazy but it feels like he is a part of me. My father was everything in the world to me and we were so much alike, it's unbelievable. Our ways are very similar. We are, of course, very fiery and snappy and that can be a good and a bad thing. We both would give our heart and our word, of course, and we would also argue a great deal with each other being so much alike, but love would come through in the end, always winning any battles of ego we might have. I would say to him after an argument, "I should not have done that. I should not have argued with you."
He would then say, "Oh no, Patrick, don't say that, that's our way of life. You have always got to argue with your son," he would say, "that's the best part about being me and you." he

would say.

I am not sure I could ever be more than half a man as my father, just the way it is, he was such a hard man to follow. Everything he had on him was nice, well cut and always well presented, it was his way. He only ever wore the one ring, a big diamond ring, it wouldn't be cheap, it always had to be a good diamond ring of quality, that's all he would ever wear, a statement of solidity in itself. He loved the style they offered up, the cut and style of them matched his clothing along with his shoes and his hair. He even had a Rolex when no one else had them, I say he had them well over fifty years ago. They would be worth an absolute mint in these days.

I remember, we would often go off in the car driving for hours, and we would have such great laughs together. Fantastic fun always. To me, I always remember my father as being an outstanding, good-looking man, his hair was coal black, a fine body of a man.

I would say the Old Queen was the spine of the family, that's the truth of it. She was the spine behind my father, everything my father worked for, was for her. They suited each other so much it was like a tailor had knit them together – well-made and matched in life and Earth and now matched in Heaven.

She really did appear like a queen to us, fantastic hair, diamonds, great clothing, immaculate looking like the Queen, except she was our queen. She really was a fox of a woman, so very smart with the money, putting it away for the future, a really intelligent and clever woman. I remember, she would walk to the pub with us, and all the other women would be there, drinking like fish, drinking anything put in front of them. She would only ever have one half of lager and that would do her the whole night, on the odd occasion having a gin and tonic. A proper lady she was.

I loved her so much, she was like my mother. My real mother gave birth to me, my mother is my whole world to me, but Lizzy Doyle became my mother when my real mother wasn't there. I loved her so much, she really was a lovely, lovely lady in the truest sense of the word.

She was so clever and so brainy and what a good-looking woman she was; coal-black hair, black skin. She was like an Italian-looking lady, such elegance in her dress, she used to dress just so beautifully, I swear people used to come over all the time and ask her where she got her clothes made, or where she would buy them from. She had jewellery and I am not joking when I say this, you would think it was Elizabeth Taylor's rings and earrings, but it was all real, all proper diamonds, gold and silver, the best. Such incredible style she had about her. She used to wear rings that you would go blind looking at, diamonds that were pure pink and blue, out of this world, hardly any gold on them, pure DIAMONDS.

I remember once, five-pound pieces were all the rage and she would have a chain with five-pound pieces on it, hundreds of them, she had a bracelet with twenty pounds hanging out of it, just full of two-pound pieces and sovereigns and all that.

If she could ever do you a good turn, she would do it for you and not tell anybody that she had helped you in any way. If she lent someone money no one would ever know it. It was always just between the two of them. She would not tell a soul. God only knows how many people she lent money to and how much was owed to her when she died.

My, my, as sure as I live and breathe, she was a good-looking woman and she wore all this with sheer style. I can see her now, just thinking about her, full of great looks, charisma, talent, charm, oozing with personality, a fine, kind, generous and brilliant woman to me, to others and above all else, to my father.

She lived twelve months from the day my father died. She just wanted to see the headstone on my father's grave and when she had seen that in place, she went in peace to be with him. I still believe with all my heart, that she died of a broken heart and couldn't bear to be without my father any longer. Two days after she died the two of them had the headstone to share together. What a woman! I always called her my 'Old Queen'. My mother is everything to me, my life, but my Old Queen was called the right name and had a special place in my heart. She certainly had the right name.

She never got above herself with the wealth that she had or anything like that, she was so down to earth, you would think she had nothing, that's also the way my father was in so many ways. They never lost who they came from and what they were. They came from wagons, and it's an honour to say that they kept their culture and their history and carried it with them with pride. That's why I am honoured to say I am so very proud of my father and I'm also so proud of the Old Queen.

My father would never buy her any nonsense, it had all to be the very best and real quality, well made, well designed, the best. He had a name like a racehorse, a thoroughbred and so his woman had to have the very best, so she did, always.

To sum up my Old Queen, she was truly a good woman, an outstanding woman, who loved me for truth, I would go back and tell my real mother about my visits and she would naturally be worried over me when I was young. I would tell my mother that she loved me the Old Queen with all her heart, I am her son too, and so she was my mother as I was her son too. She never gave birth to me but I was her son, I know that for a fact, she never gave birth to me but she was my mother in so many ways. She was my Old Queen, my mother is Maggie Ward, there is no woman above my mother, she is my life, but the Old Queen, I loved her, I loved her – she was very dear to me, very kind to me, but then again you would hope you would be dear and kind to your son because that's what it was like out of all the sons, she said this to me, "You know Patrick," the Old Queen would say, "You are my older son you know?"

I would say, "Of course I am Lizzie."

"Stop calling me Lizzie," she would say jokingly.

"Sorry, my Old Queen!" I would reply, that's how beautiful it was.

I remember once doing something very wrong a long time ago and my sisters backed me up all the way. They were there to support and help me no matter what. They had love for me as I had for them, a truly, deep love no matter what.

People often say to me, "Why are you and Martin so close to each other?" We have been together since I was seven years of age and from that point on, we never really left each other. So, we understood each other as fighters and as people me and Martin and when we got married, we did it together, what a day that was!

Two brothers married two sisters, on the same day, just fantastic, it was etched on my memory like yesterday. When we had children, they became double first cousins, like brothers they were, and it was a fine thing to watch as they grew together and of course one sister.

We had the most tragedy in all of this, our two oldest sons died together, alongside one of their other cousins. That day is etched on my brain as if it happened yesterday. So, me and Martin had a bond, a bond that could not be broken, brought about by the death of our own dear sons.

My brother Martin, my lovely brother Martin was broken when his wife died, just like my Roseanne was broken hearted because it was her sister that died and she was very close to her. Martin was broken in the heart, his heart had been torn out of him, he will never be the Martin that he was. That is one of the reasons I love our Martin so much, he is totally on his own, he has two sons Patrick and Dougie and they are both very good to him.

Our Francie, God rest his lovely soul, we think of him and celebrate him too. He was our father's brains, he had the same brain as my old fella, he could look at you and tell you exactly what you were thinking. Francie was so very intelligent, it was unbelievable. I often go to London to see my other brothers; I just love it. I miss our Francie fiercely though, he was a wonderful fella who died of cystic fibrosis, he was a great fella, a real good-looking lad and he was married to a woman called Maggie Maloney. They were really happy together and she went back to her family when he died. She did find someone else and eventually got married and had kids. She married young Gussy and is very happy. Her mammy was my first cousin. Francie was years younger than me, twenty, twenty-five years younger, and I used to go to him for advice. You could talk to him, tell him your secrets and no one would ever get to know them ever. He was an old-fashioned, great, gentleman, a man of his pure word. When my father died, we knew we had to put him in Kensal Rise with the old brothers and my Old Queen knew that too.

I love all my brothers of course, our Johnny, Qe and Simey – we go back a lot of years and we've shared many a good time and bad. Then there's our Tony – he's quite short in stature, but stockily built. He could rock for fun and box for fun. Our Barney, he loved hare coursing and fighting chickens, a great man. I love them all, so much. Then there was our Charlie who I also loved dearly – he was a good-looking man, he was, God rest his soul. I do miss my brother David though. We had a falling out some time ago, but I'll tell you this on God's honest truth – I will give him one almighty hug one day – mountains may never meet, but men surely will and I will see him again and I will hug him.

I can't forget about my sisters; I adore them all too. Angela was my older sister on my father's side and I loved her so very much. I adored and loved my sister Mary, I loved her more than she would have ever known. My sister Kate, a handsome woman indeed. Then my sister Julie who I always loved with all my heart and soul.

The best thing that ever happened to me in my whole life is my wife, Roseanne, without her I think I'd be dead now, no, I don't think it, I know it. She has saved me countless times and I am forever in awe of her. What a wonderful, loving, understanding, tolerant, beautiful woman she is! My Roseanne is my heart and soul. She is my better half, she is. To me, she is as good looking today as she was the day we met, over forty years ago. She has had to put up with a lot over the years, because I can be a bit of a flirt with people, I am a bit of a braggard with her at times, how I wish I wasn't. I once made a mistake in my life but never again. Of course, she has also had her own problems as well, everyone has demons and those are her stories to tell, not mine. There's been a lot of tragedy in her family; her Mummy, Daddy, brother, her beautiful sister, when they died it really hurt Roseanne very badly.

I am the proud father of ten children with my beautiful, lovely wife Roseanne. As you know, we've had our own tragedies in this respect with losing some of our babies and we lost our Patrick later on in life which was devastating to us. So, we have left with us on this Earth, Simey, David, Johnny, Martin-Tom and Margaret. I had five sons, only four now though and I love them dearly and I guess they love me back. My daughter, Margaret, being my only girl, I adore as anyone with only one daughter will understand.

You think that when your family has grown up, that you will no longer have problems – erm no – that's when your worries start! When your children are young and in their beds under your roof, you don't realise how happy you really are. You do have worries now and then , you know, making ends meet, giving the children everything they need, making sure they are happy and as carefree as possible. But once they grow up and leave that bed and leave home, then your real worry starts.

I have sons that have my heart broke, because I worry about them, as much as they think that you don't, I worry about them all the time. My Simey, David, Johnny, my Martin-Tom and my main worry is my daughter Margaret.

My son Simey, he's doing well, he's doing very well, thank God per Jesus, he's doing very well. He has his own business up and running now and he makes chalets and mobile homes. He is happily married to Donna and they have seven sons including little baby Qe, who is gorgeous and has Down's syndrome. He is a fox though, real brainy, he has all the other boys beat to death and killed, murdered by his brains!

My son David, he has been naughty, he got sent to prison. My David has got three girls, just beauty queens every one of them.

My son Johnny is like a rollercoaster – you got him now, then you haven't got him tomorrow, up and down, over and under, he is a moody blue. My Johnny has two sons and four girls.

My son Martin-Tom, thank God he is married and living happily up in Scotland. My Martin-Tom has one little boy.

Margaret obviously had five brothers but no sisters. I think it's been harder for her, on her own like that. She is very, very, special to me; she has to be – she's the only daughter I have. Then all of a sudden, my daughter Margaret was having problems with her husband. He used to come back from wherever he had been and every couple of days, he would give her a beating. He would be out of his head with drugs and drink and then he wouldn't remember it.

I wake up one day, Margaret has come over to see me and she's got a 'bottle' face, it was a sad day, just horrendous to see her like that and this went on for years and years, then one day she came to me and she says the one thing that makes your heart sing. She said to me, "I am divorcing him, Daddy."

I nearly jumped over the moon I was so relieved. I said to her, "Are you sure, Maggie? I've kept it from your mum, she has no idea what he has done to you, and I don't want to upset her, but it's the children you have to think about now. Are you sure?"

My Margaret ended up getting divorced, it's just one of them things in life, it happens, love just evaporated as it does when you're in those circumstances day-in, day-out, and they decided in the end that it was better for the children to divorce. About three to four years after she met another fella called John, he's a Scottish fella and I think he is one of the nicest chaps in the world. He treats my Margaret like royalty, VIP treatment, red carpet, every minute and it works vice versa, she thinks he is a king, she loves him with all her heart and treats him the same. I am grateful because John has two boys and my Margaret has three girls and one boy and both of them love each other's children the same, what a gift.

Now it does not end there, my ex-son-in-law got a new girlfriend who he ended up marrying. You know, I realise he'd been in a black place, a dark, dark place and it's not a nice place to be in, I know from my own experiences. So I'm happy for him, that he's sorted himself out and he is also a lovely man now. He needs someone in his life to love and to love him back. Everyone should be loved, it is a normal part of life, but it also a gift you shouldn't squander if you are lucky enough to be in a loving relationship. Just to hear the words 'I love you, so much' and to say them back and show your love through your actions is just the best feeling in the world. Me and John, my ex son-in-law, we get on better now than we ever got on before. Ain't that funny? We got on well for years, but then the trouble started, he fell into the drugs and drink and treated my Margaret very badly. That will put the kibosh on any friendliness, won't it? However, he is reformed now and we get on okay. He is once again a lovely man and I hope God minds him. His children are my life, all my grandchildren are my life, but Margaret's children are very special to me and she's happy again now.

My main thought in life is my family, that my children and grandchildren are safe, that is everything!

I have so many grandchildren I often get myself mixed up but I am so very blessed. I am lucky enough to be very close to them all, I love all my grandchildren. Your grandchildren become your own children, somehow you can show your grandchildren lots more precious love, because as you get older you are less busy and have more time for them and of course you pick them up but you can then put them out and give them back when you are tired! Not that I ever really want to give them back of course.

I have, of course, lots of daughters and sons in law and they are family as well. Donna has been with us since she was sixteen, so she is really close.

I love all of my family but sometimes I struggle to love myself, I love to do things for other people and now know how important it is to love yourself too but I do struggle with it. When I find myself doing things for other people I get real pleasure from it, I just love it to see the smile on their faces when you have helped out in the best way you can. The harder the task that I must do for them, the greater my sense and feeling of achievement. My philosophy is if you can help someone, you should, and when I do, it just makes me feel so good and makes my day. I do not think of myself as being better than anyone else for being like this, it's good for us all to help others, as it helps ourselves. Try it, honestly, see how it makes you feel, I bet you agree! As I have already said this is the greatest thing to come out of being a so-called celebrity, charity, caring and doing stuff for others is my greatest gift to myself.

## _My Roseanne_

I have been married for forty-five years now and it's like I married my Roseanne just yesterday.

To me, my Roseanne has got better looking as we have both got older. She looks young, she is beautiful and always gorgeous, takes care of her appearance very well indeed and she is always sixteen to me. We may get old, body wise, but brain, heart and soul wise, she is always stunning. There is no one like your woman, no one above your partner once chosen in life, swans forever!

A few years back, me and my woman were having a good old argument and it would be fair to say that I had drunk too much that day. I had forgotten to get home on time and I really was drunk, not happy to admit it, but it was the truth. This argument was a full-on row that sometimes only a man and wife can have, it was war! So anyhow, I eventually went to bed and when I woke up the next morning there is not a sight nor sound of Roseanne to be seen or heard!

One day goes by, nothing. Two days went by, nothing. Three days and nothing to be seen or heard. Eventually, we are up to five days and I am worried sick, not a smell of her, gone! I was fully convinced that, as is often in our culture, that she would have gone to her mother or father, or to her brother or sisters for a while, after this big argument. Eventually, I went to her mum's place, nothing, same story when I visit her sister, eventually I get to her brother's and ask him, "Where is Roseanne?" I asked, half desperate.

"She's not here," he said.

"I can see she is not here but where is she? Where is my woman? I want her and I want her now!" I was getting pretty angry by this point, chasing my tail around and not getting anywhere.

"Look Paddy, Roseanne is in the Canary Islands," he told me.

"What!" I said.

"She has taken your credit card."

"Oh my," I said, "I knew the credit card was gone."

"Well, she's got your credit card and her and Martin-Tom have gone there and they'll be back by the end of the week."

So, I said to him, "Fair enough, don't worry about it."

So, time passes and she is there a full week. Now she has my credit card and I know she is going to hurt me; she is going to put a big hole in this credit card all right!

The week goes by and still no sign of her. Then I am in this hotel, meeting friends and I bump into a few Travellers, who say to me, "Hey Paddy, I saw your wife today,"

"What?" I said, "Where? Where did you see her?"

"She's in the Hilton Hotel," which was across the road from where I was.

"She's what?" I said in disbelief. Well, I did not let him know that she had gone away and I said to him, "Okay, thanks," telling him I would catch up with him later.

I flew straight across the road to the Hilton Hotel early in the morning. Now in the bar, the lift is right next to it and to go to the exit she would have to come this way out, past where I was waiting, this was the only way out. So, I sat down and started to wait. The morning passes and afternoon is well on its way and I had been there for ages, waiting for her to come by. I am wondering if this information I'd been given was wrong and the next minute the door opens and there she is with Martin-Tom, a lovely, pink top and a pink skirt on her and a pair of nice slippers.

'OH MY GOD!' I thought, she looks handsome, so very, very handsome indeed. She had a golden colour, a stunning bronze look about her, glorious, not just because she was my wife, she looked simply amazing. 'Look at that woman,' I thought to myself, 'she is something else!'

"Hello Roseanne," I said, and we started to talk.

"You know I've been away?" she said, "I have been on holiday."

"I heard that," I said.

"Yeah," she said, "me and my Martin-Tom."

Well, we started to get into another few words, as things were not yet resolved.

"You took my credit card!" I said.

Then Martin-Tom says, "Mummy, let's have another holiday, let's leave Daddy and go away again."

"I am going to kill you, Martin-Tom!" I heard myself saying in the heat of the row. "You you're a sausage, don't do anything like that again, you should have phoned me up." I said to him.

"Well look Daddy, next time you have an argument again, me and Mummy will go away, won't we Mummy?" My son says to me all cocky like.

"Yes, we are, Martin-Tom, we are!" said Roseanne.

Now by this time I am totally furious. Eventually I said to Roseanne, "let me get you a drink," and she agreed, so we grabbed a couple of drinks from the bar and sat down. We started to have a little banter as husband and wives sometimes do and she had a twinkle in her eye.

"So, Roseanne, I've always wanted to know what the rooms were like in the Hilton," now don't forget, I am already paying for this room with my credit card. I know that she has gone the *Full Monty*, the liqueurs, the luxuries, breakfast in bed, wine etc. you name it, it's on my credit card.

"Oh Paddy," she said, with a wry smile, "you would not believe it, they are lovely, lovely rooms, definitely five-star, top-class," she said.

"Give us a look upstairs then," I said.

"No," she said, "you just want to get into the room."

"Look," I said, with a big jokey smile, "at the end of the day, I am paying for it, so I wouldn't mind a little look." She started to laugh with mischief in her eyes and that old familiar look of love and a real attractive smile. I started to laugh even more and so did she and Martin-Tom.

"All right then," she said, "you can have a quick look at the room and then you will have to leave."

"Of course I will!" I said, the twinkle now in my eye.

"You had better leave," she said.

"Oh, I will, don't worry," I promised.

We all went up in the elevator to take a look at the room. We went in and the room was out of this world, something else indeed, at a good price, no doubt, sheer luxury.

"Wow! This is the best!" I said.

"Yeah, it's nice ain't it Paddy?" she said.

Happiness is being content. To me happiness is everything in content. I'm not ashamed to say this but I wish I was that. Why would you say that I hear you say? I strike most people as being happy and I am happy but everyone, no matter who you are, everyone's got problems. They have skeletons in their closet. Ever since I lost Patrick, I've never done no good out of it. And I've already or always screwed up in one way or another so… my happiness now in my life, is my grandchildren. That's how I know I'm getting old. I've got, oh my, I should be ashamed of myself, I don't even know how many I've got. I've got a load anyway, I know that! Between twenty to forty, honestly, it's a lot. Well, let's put it this way, my Simey's got six boys, my Janet's got four, no hang on, Janet's got five, maybe six, but let's say five. David has got three, Margaret's got five, my Martin-Tom has got one, now, who else am I missing? They are all on the site with me and Roseanne. Round the corner.

If you've got something to bank and you're not dying of hunger, then you've nothing to worry about. You can look like you've got thousands and thousands of pounds but you haven't. How you present yourself and how you look and act, tells people how happy you are, so I'm content with the way life is now.

I'm very happy right now but the future… well… the future's going to be a bad world and all I want for me and the family is peace. As you get older, all you want in life is peace. And you should have peace. Leave me alone, leave my children alone and just get on with your own life. Because fair fighting has finished now, everything is guns and cutting people up and smashing things up. So that life's not fair, it was never fair for me anyhow, I did what I had to do, years ago now and it's two different things, it's like chalk and cheese and I'm a completely different person now, oh completely different, but when I say I'm a completely different person, I'm not a completely different man!

## _Prejudice_

Travellers get a lot of stick, a real lot of stick, far too much. I remember when I was a wee boy, and this is the truth. It was all too common to see signs in pub windows and other places saying, 'NO DOGS – NO GYPSIES – NO BLACKS'. That is something I will never, ever forget. That is how we were often thought of by some, as animals, along with black people, being treated the exact same way. Now of course, that was a long time ago, but it is something that stays with you and you never forget.

I remember if we were getting towed off a site where we had camped up, we would always get a slap off the police, honestly this is the truth, it seemed like it was as regular as clockwork, we were getting slapped by the police. It is the way we were treated, some people just thought we were nothing, we were just rubbish! I used to think to myself that it was all over, that it was so many years ago and in the past.

I think prejudice towards Travellers comes from people's perceptions of how we've been raised or reared. I remember being at a function with a few people, no names, but I loved this person's accent, it was really posh, but they said to me, "Oh, I say, you're not half as bad as I thought you would be! I thought you were scum!"

I gave this person a certain look if you know what I mean? As if to say, I don't know what's wrong with them, but it's just what they've heard or gotten used to and it's wrong, so very wrong. Now don't forget, that when I was small, I'd go to school, I'd go in the class and sit in the corner, into a corner – that was my day, and you're looked at like, you're smelly, you're dirty, you're scruffy. And that's most people's opinions.

Now I live in North Wales at Queensferry and it is the loveliest place in the whole wide world, and I mean that, the loveliest place you could ever wish to go to.

There are three pubs that I used to go to around where I live, each of them was run by a landlady, I won't name them but they are all part of a thing called *'Pub Watch'*. You've probably heard of it, but at the time I had no idea what it was or what it meant, until it was used against me. We were in one of the pubs one day, as a very dear friend of mine had lost his little girl, she had died at only two years of age. We went to the

Pub with him for a few drinks to help him and chat to him, but he was losing it a bit due to all the stress and pain. Suddenly, the landlady says, "I can't serve you people anymore."

I remember it well and if there is one thing I am very aware of, it is prejudice, for obvious reasons and it hurts my heart so much when people use the expression, 'YOU PEOPLE – YOU LOT – YOU GYPSIES' and so on.

So, I said to her, "My darling, listen to me, forgive me, forgive me for calling you darling, it's just a figure of speech. My friend over there has just lost his child, his little girl. She was only two years old. Please, he's allowed to blow a little steam, please don't worry about him he's harmless enough and I'll take care of him."

All he had done was to take a packet of nuts off the bar without thinking, that's all he had done, not with any malintent, he just wasn't thinking straight given what had happened to him. I think the nuts were worth about thirty pence! Now, this man had been a regular in the pub and had spent a lot of money there and I mean a lot. This landlady suddenly, for no reason whatsoever, becomes completely irrational and the situation escalates.

She said in a shaky voice, "I am getting the police to you people!"

I said, "Excuse me darling, how dare you say, 'US PEOPLE' to us in that way?"

I just cannot stand the misuse of that word, it stayed with me from the past and I will not stand by and be mistreated in that way for myself or anyone else, for no reason at all.

"HOW DARE YOU USE THOSE WORDS THAT WAY!" I shouted. "Would you say: 'YOU BLACKS', 'YOU INDIANS', 'YOU WHATEVER'? Would you? Would you say that to them? No, you wouldn't, would you?"

I could feel myself getting very upset… "Don't ever say that again in that way!" I said to her.

"I am getting the police!" She said to me.

"My darling, go ahead and get the police," I said, "go ahead and get them." Hoping that she would. Because to be fair, we had done absolutely nothing wrong and bringing in the police would have been very embarrassing for her. Of course, no police or anyone else came. We stayed, she carried on serving us, we behaved well and we were there until closing time, just supporting my friend in his hour of need. When the final bell rang, we finished our drinks, I put the empty glasses on the bar and we left. No trouble. No misbehaviour, just a little bit of emotion escaping out from time to time, which was totally normal and to be expected in the circumstances.

The next day I decided I would pop back into the pub to see the landlady, you know, take her a nice card in and apologise for the nut incident and maybe talk to her about how Travellers are stereotyped and treated badly and how, when someone does that, how it makes me feel. She wasn't there though, so I gave the card to one of the bar workers, told them I was sorry about the previous night, but that the man with us was upset because he had just lost his child and I offered to pay for the nuts.

He said to me, "That's very kind of you Paddy, and listen, you have known the man a long time and he didn't really do anything wrong. To smooth things over though, would you mind, Paddy, keeping him and yourself out of here just for a week, to let things all calm down?"

For the sake of peace, I agreed. We weren't barred and we hadn't done anything wrong in reality but I felt that this would help to sort things out for us all and that was that.

Now on my life and this is the truth, about six or seven months after that happened, I went to another pub in

Queensferry that was one of the three I told you of. I had never been in this pub in my life, me, Martin and my brother Dudlow go into the pub and I said to the person behind the bar, "Can I get three pints please?" Pulling out a fifty-pound note.

"I can't change that," she said.

"That's okay, don't worry about it love, I will go to the shop next door and buy something to change it." I said back to her.

"You won't get it changed there," she said.

"I will, don't be worrying. I'll go get it changed, if you would please fill them pints for me, I'll be right back?" I said.

So, off I goes across the road and into the post office and they changed the fifty-pound note for me straight away. I came back into the pub and says, "There you are," to the lady behind the bar.

Now I noticed an old man and woman in the corner on their own and I asked them if they would like a drink. I felt I might be able to help them a little as he was on sticks and she was in a wheelchair. My upbringing taught me to look after and respect the older folk. So, we had a bit of a chat and I got him a pint and she fancied just a half, so I ordered them up and they were delighted.

Me, Martin and Dudlow sat down, just the three of us and I noticed two country lads, ordinary folk just playing a friendly game of pool. Not many in the pub at all. Just normal people having a couple of drinks, minding their business and enjoying each other's company. It was lovely until I noticed out of the corner of my eye, that the landlady was on the phone, chatting away to someone, but she kept glancing over towards me and my brothers. It was just a quick glance over, then her eyes would turn towards the ground and she would turn her back to us. Each time this happened, her scowls got deeper and deeper, she was looking at us like we were devils and demons. I can read people well and knew by the way she was scowling, something was 'up' and it was not good. I said to my brothers "What's wrong with the woman? Can you see the way she is looking at us with fire and mistrust in her eyes?"

I waved at her from the corner we were sitting in and asked, "Is everything all right?"

"Yep, yep," she says, waving back but while she's still on the phone. Her cheeks were changing colour before our eyes, a red blush rising up from her neck and over her cheeks. I could just hear her saying, "Right then, I am not serving them lot then."

One of the boys playing pools says, "Hey don't call them that – '*them lot*'!"

"I didn't call them 'them lot'," she said, "I said, them people." She basically used the words in exactly the same way as the woman in the previous pub did, where the problems started over the nuts and it was driving me NUTS! It was pure racism to me – plain and simple – prejudice, it was very clear what she really meant. I walked up to the bar, not wanting trouble or anything but not wanting to be abused or to allow anyone else to be abused.

"Excuse me," I said, "would you not call us that way! We are human beings just like yourself, we are just the same as you, we are humans and just as good as you!"

"Right, I want you out, the lot of you – go on now – get out!" She snapped back.

"Now hold on lady," I said to her, trying to control my underlying hurt.

"I don't want you in here no more," she said, with a real nasty look on her face.

Well fair play to them the two young chaps playing pool, one of them says, "Hang on a minute, you can't be saying things like that, 'YOU LOT', 'YOU PEOPLE', you can be done for that!"

It felt so good to have them onside.

"I don't care," she said, while still on the phone, wanting her boyfriend, partner or other landlady she was on the phone to, to hear all the abuse she was giving us.

In the meantime, I had decided to put my phone on record, just to be safe. I was totally sick of being treated like this for no good reason and I wanted to make sure, that if the police did end up coming out, I had evidence that the abuse was only coming from one place – her, not me. She shouted back, "I am getting the police!"

I said, "You go ahead and get the police, I would like them here anyhow. I'm going to have you now for the way you have just talked to us and also we have two independent fellas here who can verify what you have just done!"

"What's your name?" She asked.

"I'm Paddy Doherty," I said, "and I am here with my brothers and we are going to wait here until the police come and we shall tell them everything you have just said!"

175

Of course, she didn't call the police. I guess she knew she was in the wrong on this one. The mood had definitely dropped in temperature, so we eventually drank our pints and quietly left, but as we were going, I said, "When the police come, let them know we are in the pub next door please." Now I did record it all and the two fellas gave us their name and numbers as we left.

Four weeks later, a police officer comes to my door and gives me a letter in my hand. He tells me I am on a *Pub Watch* for ten years!

I said to the police officer, "What's a *Pub Watch*? I've never heard of such a thing as a *Pub Watch*. Do you want me to go and watch a pub or something?"

He started to chuckle to himself, and I just looked at him, wondering what he'd found so funny. Was he making fun of me?

"No Paddy, *Pub Watch* was set up as a voluntary thing where some pubs in an area try to tackle and prevent anti-social behaviour and have agreed to report anti-social behaviour and criminal activity. It's there to promote a sense of security for customers and staff. If a pub is registered as a Pub Watch pub, then if just one pub in the group has any trouble of any kind, they tell the other pubs and that means the person is barred from all the pubs in the *Pub Watch* group. And… that means for you, you can't go into these pubs until ten years is up. You are not allowed to go into the pub for at least the next ten years, or any of these other nine pubs on the list, I'm afraid."

Now eight of these pubs I had never ever been in, but two of the pubs mentioned were the two pubs I have been telling you about where the landladies had asked us to leave.

"Now hold on a minute," I said to the police officer, "Was there any police called to these pubs over me?"

"No," he said.

"Was I involved in any fighting?"

"No," he said again.

"Did I shout and scream at anyone?"

"No." he said, "not as far as we know you didn't Sir."

So, I told him everything that had happened and offered him the details of the young chaps that had witnessed everything, but he cut me short and said, "Listen Paddy, it's the first time I have ever seen anyone get a ten-year *Pub Watch* ban! Listen, you have been great here, you have been great with the community and you always keep the peace, so just take note of this and don't break the ruling, okay?"

My thoughts on this were, there should be a human rights in this, you should be able to go and defend yourself, go to a meeting and put your side of the story. You know maybe a meeting where the bad things that have been said against are discussed and you can go and explain things. No, nothing, just a letter sent to me via a police officer, *Pub Watch* – ten years – WOW! How racist and how biased it has all been. This was not a barring for twelve months but for ten years, I was so insulted. I had actually done lots of appearances for pubs in my local area, you know for charity work and the like, suddenly all of them taking the word of two people and getting me banned for TEN YEARS! This really hurt, the injustice made me boil. On the word of these people, with not one word of defence from me I am sentenced, and it just felt so very wrong. I know everyone where I live, the butchers, barbers, bakers, loads of people and I have never had any problems, ever, so this really hurt.

I remember telling my psychiatrist, Miss Winter, about it all and she said, "That is appalling, I will write a letter for you if you like?" Which she did.

As it stands, I am still waiting to hear and get this matter resolved, but it is so wrong and an example of what still goes on in the prejudiced minds of some people and the misuse of power when they have it to abuse.

It cannot be right that you get on a *Pub Watch* on someone else's say without having a chance to defend yourself, it's pure wrong. It's injustice of any kind that makes me boil! NO police, NO violence, nothing, just someone's word and your ability to live in society like anyone else is taken away. JUST WRONG!

I still go to pubs nearby and have a regular place, it's great to socialise and meet nice, honest people. I remember one day, certain Travellers came into the pub who I knew would order a lot of drinks, with no intention to pay for any of them. I was watching them. The landlord came over to me and said, "Look Paddy, I don't want any trouble but they have ordered drinks and won't pay for them. Anything you can do to help me out here?"

"Leave that to me," I said.

I walked over to the group and said to them, "Now boys, you've ordered some drinks, just pay for them, okay?"

One of the group said, "We are going now Paddy."

"That's fine if you are going but you pay for the drinks you've had before you leave." I said to them in a quiet tone. They got my message and paid what they owed before they left.

Before the likes of Tyson, Saunders and myself, many people I felt, thought of Travellers as scum, dirt and vomit. I understand how black people, Indians, Asians and others feel, because so many people are racist against us, just as much as they are against them. It's deeply upsetting and a great shame. We are just people, all of us and we have all got the same things going on in our lives.

One of the reasons, I guess Travellers are so very protective of their families, is due to the racism we encounter every day. I am not saying that to attack other people, it's not meant in a bad way at all, there is good and bad in all types of people, just as much as there is good and bad in any community of Travellers and others alike. As we would say there are some bowsies in Travellers, some bowsies in white, black, Indian and Asian people or any of others but there is also some real gentlemen and ladies amongst everyone. English, Irish Welsh or Scots, even amongst Traveller people, everyone, we are all the same. No matter what race they are, who they are, or what they do. If your child falls in love with someone, be they black, blue, pink, orange, green, yellow with red spots on, if it's what makes them happy, if they love that person, they'll love them no matter their colour, race, creed or religion, we have to wish them all the luck in the world and support them in their decisions. After all, that's how we learn and become better people.

Who is anyone to throw a stone at anyone else? Before they throw any stones at anyone, they should look over their own shoulder before throwing that stone and see if someone might throw a stone at them!

As I have already described, my mother and father were together for a while when I was born but eventually, they split up. That is life sometimes, my father went his way and my mother hers. So, when I was born, I was black, I was as black as coal, I looked like any other black baby. People would come to see my mother and me of course, now you have to remember that this was sixty-one years ago.

People would say, "Oh, she had a child from a black man!" Now at that time, I am sorry to say, this was seen as a complete scandal amongst Travellers and anyone. Thank God times have moved on and we have woken up!

My father was a very dark-skinned man, on his side my sisters and a couple of my brothers are very, very dark too. Johnny is dark, our Barney is, so is Francie, my sister Kate is dark and also Lizzie's dark and of course, Mary is dark as well as Margaret. So nearly all my father's side are dark but people did not make allowances for that and because he was not around, I guess some of them loved the gossip and the scandal at that time, just sheer prejudice about the colour of our skin.

Even now, when the sun comes out, I go really dark, it's part of my genetic past and inherited genes from our Romany forebearers, I would guess. When I was growing up many a people would say to me, "Ah, the black bastard's here," or "Hey, black bastard…," for no reason at all, other than I was a bit darker than them. In time, you get so used to it, that it stops bothering you, when you are young and you hear this every day of the week, it eventually becomes water off a duck's back to you. I look back now and I realise how awful this was, how I became so degraded by it that it stopped me from being able to develop a little bit of respect for myself. If you are exposed to this for years and years from an early age, sadly it becomes a part of your life.

These days if I hear people calling names of any kind, I find I get quite upset, it's so degrading and disgusting, it's one of the reasons I hate racism of any kind. To use this language against people is one of the most disgusting behaviours in the world, particularly when the person is not able to defend themselves.

I really feel so sorry for my mother, seeing her go through all that in the years that followed my birth and so much of her life. As an adult, seeing this would break my heart for her, but as a child, I could do nothing to defend her. How painful it must have been for her to put up with this vile nonsense, what a woman she is. I can say this as a man, no one is allowed to insult my mother ever again.

How long are Travellers going to have to hide their identity to get work? To go out and make a living? I know a lot of young girls and boys who called up recruitment agencies to find work and they hide what they are, even where they live sometimes, because even now, if they've done really well and managed to find a job, there have been cases where, once the employer found out they were a Traveller, they got sacked. Oh, they did it in a clever way so there would be no come back on them, and these young ones' names are sort of blocked for jobs then, even with the recruitment agencies. It's very sad, extremely annoying and just not fair at all. These are good kids and young adults and they get my respect because a lot of Travellers won't work the nine-to-five, but these ones do want to work, so give them a break and be respectful to them.

I have always found, oh what do they call it now? Oh, that's right LGBTQ+ people to be some of the most welcoming, friendly people in the world, totally accepting of them I am. It's the King, the Queen, the Jack, the Ace of Spades they're the best! Ha-ha, I'm only having a laugh, all people are human, good or bad, it's just life. We are all people. A person doesn't ask to be of a certain sexuality, do they? You are what you are – end of. We are born to be who and what we are and we should all be able to accept these things as they are. Me and Roseanne, a man and a woman, heterosexuals or straight (or whatever, you want to call it) love each other. LGBTQ+ (or whatever you want to call it) love each other too – no difference and that's what we should be focusing on – Love – not Hate!

What you are, is what you are, be happy and love each other that's the thing. It is what it is, accept life no matter who you are or what you are, don't fight, accept yourself, accept life as it is and live as yourself, accept yourself for what you are – that is how I view it! I have seen a lot of people being abused over the years for being LGBTQ+ and just like racism it is a prejudice and it is WRONG.

I simply cannot bear anyone who slags of LGBTQ+ people of any kind, it's simply wrong. Why would people slag them off, they didn't ask to be who they are and who is the person to slag them off? No one is above you. You are no better a person than anyone else to judge them in any way. We all need to accept people for who they are, what they are and how they are without judgement!

The world will be a much better place when we all learn that. Me and my Roseanne have learned this and we are all the better for it, we have been married for forty-five years now and it's like I married my Roseanne just yesterday.

## *Charity ... or is it?*

The greatest thing that ever happened to me and I mean this in the whole world. The greatest thing that happened to me, to come out of this celebrity madness is the charity work I have been able to do.

From being a young fella, a child I suppose, I always wanted to be able to do things for charity and I always wanted to find a good way to help other people. I used to think how can I do this? How can I get to help people in a real, good way? But I just didn't really know how in those days. I don't know if it's something about being a Traveller we never seem to get into organised things or know how to meet people who work in organisations like registered charities.

After I had done all the TV shows, *Big Fat Gypsy Wedding*, *When Paddy Met Sally*, *Celebrity Big Brother* etc. with all these other famous people and all that, I found to my delight that charities started coming to me and asking me to make various appearances.

Now you don't get paid for this, nor should you in my opinion, I found myself doing a lot for cancer charities, women and men, prostate charity, lots and lots of different ones. I would get asked to do loads of different appearances for so many different ones and I loved to do them and still do. It gave me such a wonderful feeling of satisfaction and I felt privileged to know that just by being there I was helping.

The wealth means nothing to me, the celebrity nonsense really doesn't matter, what does matter is the charity work I'm able to do and I love that, I love to be able to make other people happy. Driving hundreds of miles paying for the hotel and just being able to do it is the happiest thing in the world to be able to help these charities for people with prostate cancer, battered women, underprivileged children, it's the best possible thing that's ever happened along with my wife and my family.

I really could not believe how great it was for me to be able to do this, such a wonderful feeling of satisfaction to know just by being there I was able to help, a real privilege.

I remember doing one in Whitehaven. I will never forget it,

they phoned me up and said, "Paddy, would you do a charity appearance for us in Whitehaven for deprived children?"

I said, "Yes, of course, I would love to do it."

"You'll have to stay overnight."

I said, "Don't worry, I will sort it all out and I will do everything."

It took me about three hours to drive there on the day and when I arrived, I found myself at the big social club. Well, I get in there and have a warm greeting from the organisers, then the next minute a few children come in, followed by more and more and very soon there were about a hundred children (with guardians) in this hall.

I just love children from the bottom of my heart, I think children are very special, all angels full of hope, purity and possibility. So, we did loads of pictures with all of them, had fun, lots of autographs and happiness to be had, big smiles everywhere, it was such fun to see them all full of great happiness.

So, then they said, "Paddy, we would like you to go into this boxing ring and the children will spar with you, while you let them beat you and they have fun!" They were only small children I need add. So, I get in the ring with them and pretended to be beaten up with these youngsters one by one, what a laugh we all had, such a joy to see their faces as they beat me to bits, all the while laughing their heads off and having great fun.

The smiles on those kids' faces were the most beautiful thing in the world, the whole place was full of giggles as they delivered each punch and I fell on my back begging for mercy. Just brilliant fun! It's a day that will never leave me. It cost me nothing, just being there having fun and seeing their little faces filled with glee, what a gift it was to me.

Afterwards, I asked the man and woman who had put this big function on, "Why are all these children here?" They told me how all of them had been abused in one way or another or may have been homeless and actually living on the streets for a while. To me, they were just babies, it was so hurtful to hear some of the stories about their young lives.

I wondered, I thought, 'How could anyone hurt children in this way?' and I found myself bonding with these young people. It was such a privilege to make these youngsters laugh and giggle. They'd all seen me on the box, so it was a big surprise for them to be able to get to beat me up in such a fun way and it was certainly the best beating of my life. The man and the woman running the day who looked after the charity said a big thanks to me for doing it, but I assured them, the pleasure and the privilege was all mine.

Some well-known people on TV can be stuck in their own little bubbles. I think if you are doing anything for charity you should commit and do it from the heart. It has to be real and you have to be committed, you just cannot pretend that you want to be there and if you don't commit one hundred percent, then the kids or whoever you are doing the charity for, will pick up on it and they will suss out that you are doing it for the wrong reasons.

But I swear on my life, as my son has gone to God, it is the greatest gift to be able to do this for other people, the best thing to come from the whole business. I just love doing charity work.

Another charity I did some work with was in North Wales. It was for a young girl who was terminally ill. Her mother had sent me a letter telling me this young lady was in hospital and that she was coming out for the day. She was organising a special carnival for her daughter. She offered to pay me and I naturally refused because in my book, I don't believe we should be paid to do this sort of thing. In fact, I would have paid her for the privilege of going there.

I would not be paid; you should not be paid to do this sort of thing in my book.

So, this appearance for this young girl in Wales I will certainly never forget. She was very frail and in a wheelchair. I met her and gave her a kiss on the cheek and big hug and we took load of photos together. We had great fun! She has since passed away, I am sorry to say, and my memory of being with her that day will stay with me forever. She was such a lovely young lady. Moments like that, the gift to be able to bring some pleasure to someone who really deserves it, I treasure for life and that's why I feel blessed to be able to help in that way.

Someone approached me a while back and said they were organising a charity event and that, "We would split the profits."

You can imagine my response to that, cheeky bastards! Either you do something for charity, for free or you do not do it at all. Don't do something to pretend to be good, I have no time for that attitude and behaviour whatsoever. You should give your full heart and soul or just not bother.

There are other celebrities who are the same; they will do it sometimes for free if it gives them TV exposure, but most of the time they want a hefty fee. I will hold no truck with that and couldn't live with myself that way.

I remember this time I was at a function, at a really big venue, with a certain female celebrity, let's call her '*Duck*', that I've worked with before. This man came up to us and asked for a picture with us and '*Duck*' said, "NO!"
Anyway, I said to her, "Oh, come on now, '*Duck*', it's for charity, that's why we are here," and she eventually did it but she didn't really want to. Full of bullshit in other words, not truly bothered to do what I feel she should have done.

So, this man says to me, "Paddy, I am opening a venue for children to give them a safe space to go to in times of trouble or danger and it's going to be a boxing gym too. It's just a new place and we are going to open it. Would you and 'Duck' come and open it for us please?"

Straight away I said to this man, "Of course we will."

She turns round and says, "No I am not coming."

I said to her, "Come on 'Duck', it's only a small opening event, it's simple, just a few shots, it's nothing!"

"No! NO! No!" she said, "You've got to see my agent. My agent deals with all of that."

Now I knew straight away what she meant – she wanted to be paid for it and handsomely, to do it for him and the kids.


"Listen my friend," I said to the man, "You put me down for it, I will be there for you, for nothing. Put me down when you need me before and after and I do not want money!"

Looking 'Duck' in the eye, I said to the guy, "I can't do nothing with that one there, she is a sausage."

"Oi, don't call me a sausage, Paddy," she said. Well, I did not mess around, I looked her firmly in the eye and said, "YOU ARE A SAUSAGE! END OF!"


I really did not like her any more then, it just felt so wrong. Well, not that I did not like her but I did not like what she was doing. I knew then that she was false, a player as you might say. It's not that we fell out of friendship but she simply does not appear without a fee, no money, no show, no matter what the charity it seems. As they say, 'different strokes for different people.'

There are other celebrities who I might have mentioned already who are the same, they will do it sometimes for free if it gives them the TV exposure but most of the time, they want a hefty fee. Well, I will have no truck with that. I could not live with myself that way.

Almost the best pleasure for me comes when it's a small appearance and very few people know about it apart from the small group you are doing for. No press, it's the greatest pleasure then almost anonymous and seeing the joy and feeling the joy on a private appearance is just great.

I think one of the dangers of the media, when you are made famous for celebrity shows, is that people get above themselves and think they are special and deserve special treatment and payment just for being them. It does not sit well with me, we are all the same, king, queen, pauper no matter who we are just flesh on bone.

I remember one famous (so called) face coming to see me and we went for a drink. Well, this person was so full of themselves and arrogant, the owner of the pub said to me, "Paddy, he is going out now, or he is getting put out, I know he's with you so we will respect him but he leaves now!" He had upset so many people with his arrogance, yes, a bit of a celebrity with fame in his family, no more than that, so what gave him the right to behave like that with people? In the end I got so frustrated with him myself that I said to the pub owner, "You do what you want with him." His arrogance was just too much. My father was so very well known in the Traveller community, like a Rolls Royce, but I would not live on the back of his name, you make your own name and you own your own name in this life! I would never live off my father's name, never.

Do your own work, create your own name and do your charity work for the real reasons, as a charity full stop. It's the greatest honour in the world and should not be exploited in any way.

If someone said to me for example, "We want you to work in this charity shop for a day," I would do it straight up without payment, with pleasure, just knowing it puts a smile on a face.

No matter who you are or what you are, there are always people worse off than you and it's so good just to be able to make a small difference. I don't care who you are or what planet you live on, there is always someone worse off than yourself.

It's such a joy when you see the smile on a face, I love to go around to see older people and have the craic with them, you know, make them all jolly and happy.

I remember a woman in her nineties once said to me, "Oh you're so nice," she said.

"Nice! I am not nice; I am honoured for you to talk to me." I said back and I truly meant it. "Oh, you're so nice to say that," she piped back.

"Ma'am, for me to see you like that, for us to have the chat and to see your eyes glittering like diamonds, it's just wonderful, so thanks." I replied.

You know that saying, 'No one knows what happens behind closed doors.' So many children suffering in our society, getting beaten up, humiliated, bullied, threatened and abused. Of course, you can be abused in so many ways and it's not always physical but emotional or psychological. In some ways this can be worse than a beating, if you have a beating you can say, "Well I had a beating but it's over and done with," but there is a hell of a lot of children like that, even adults, men and women.

Of course, there are men getting beat up by women, it's hard to believe sometimes but it's the truth. It really opens your eyes when you do these charity appearances and you get to see and hear what is really going on.

## *Tragedy*

One of the saddest things about being a Doherty, is that we have had so much tragedy in our lives. We carry the pain when it happens and you can see it in our eyes. My father had that look.

I think we all need someone to love and treasure with all your heart, and it feels like every time I do treasure someone or love them deeply, it falls apart for me. It's like one big joke, it's not a funny joke, more like a vicious prank. It sometimes feels like something happens or will happen to people I ever love or really get close to.

When our beautiful son Patrick died in a terrible car accident at the age of eighteen, back in 1989, me and Roseanne couldn't cope with the shock and the loss. Patrick was our first-born son and I worshipped him. When he died, I wanted to die. I was ripped apart by grief. I lost the greatest thing in the world to me. Roseanne was the same. We were just lost to each other. I hate to admit it, but it almost caused the end for me and Roseanne too, as I tried to blot out the pain with drink and drugs. We had to leave, to try and get away after it all happened, trying to escape it, I guess. So, we went to Scunthorpe and stayed there, isolated from everyone, just each other for comfort and we stayed there for just under twelve months.

It was during this time that I managed to get us back to a better place again, we were so damaged by this tragedy that it was tearing us apart, we just did not know how to handle each other and be in the world without our Patrick.

At that terrible time, we had no way of coping with things, I remember near that first Christmas after Patrick's death my father came to see us. "Come up to see me for Christmas," he says, he had bought a big hotel with a big dance room in it. "Come and spend the Christmas with me."

Every Christmas for years before the tragedy, we had always gone away to a grand hotel for Christmas. I would spend a fortune to make sure the family had a great time with lots of fun and so that Roseanne didn't have the pressure of cooking all day. It used to be the happiest time of our year in so many ways, seeing the joy and happiness on the kids' faces as we handed out the presents and enjoyed being a happy family all together. So, we decided we would do this and took all the children with us. I remember, even though many of my memories are clouded of this time, that the hotel was looking so pretty; it was surrounded by deep snow that we had at the time. We thought we could help each other through it.

We were all sitting there eating Christmas dinner, the whole family and one by one we all started to cry, we just could not stop the tears from rolling. Our hearts were broken beyond belief and the pain was unbearable, our first Christmas without our dear son Patrick by our side. My dear poor wife was in a terrible state of pain and anguish and I was no good to her either, I tried to help but just failed her and I felt worse then, I just could not find the words to help her or my own pain.

I remember going up to the bar, to try and get away from the pain. My father was there with my brothers Kerry, Johnny, my brother-in-law Mikey Connors and a good few more were all drinking at the bar. They were all laughing and joking, having a great craic as we would say and who can blame them, but I just could not connect.

My head was ringing with the pain and it was like I was in a bubble, a bubble of my own Hell. I could hear myself saying in my head, 'How can anyone laugh at a time like this, don't they understand what has happened?' Life goes on of course and your own pain is not other people's pain, so it was not their fault.

I decided to go off to bed to try and escape the pain. I remember getting into bed where Roseanne was already asleep, but I found myself tossing and turning unable to switch my mind off from the anguish. I got out of bed and found myself in the corridor, walking aimlessly around, then I went back to the room and tried to sleep once more, laying there, staring up at the ceiling, with more thoughts running through my head.

I threw back the covers and found myself downstairs at the bar where they were all still drinking, laughing, and joking away. I stood in tears, watching them, I was wishing my son Patrick was still here.

My old man saw me out of the corner of his eye and came over to me. He said, "Are you all right my Patrick?"

"Old man," I said, "my heart is broken."

He put his arm around me and said, "My son, I know what it is like, I know exactly how you feel. The sons I've lost, I know your pain."

My father had lost his son Charlie when he was only thirteen years old. Both my dad and the Old Queen, his new wife, had a great deal of tragedy in their lives too, so he did understand.

"You know son, we don't mean to laugh and look like we don't care when you are in so much pain," holding me tight.

"I know," I said, "don't worry about that, it's just that my head is all over the place at this time."

"Would you come and have a drink with us?" he asked.

"You don't mind if I don't at this time?" I heard myself saying.

"No, no son, you do exactly what you feel comfortable doing," he said.

"I am just going to be walking around the hotel," I said.

"You do exactly what you want, my place is your place," he said.

"Thanks, my old man," I said. He put his arms right round me, squeezed me tight and he gave me a kiss with pure love in his heart and I did the same back.

"Old man, I needed that!" I said, "I needed that!" I slowly walked away in a haze.

When he squeezed and kissed me that time at his hotel, I knew it was love, pure love and a longing to take away my pain, the pain he had experienced himself and understood.

I found myself outside in the snow and the chilly night air, not a soul to be seen wandering around the grounds. Suddenly I heard this screaming and roaring, "WHY DID THIS HAPPEN TO ME? WHY? WHY? WHY HAS MY SON GONE? WHHHHHY?"
I realised that the shouts and cries of pain were coming from me, just echoing in the empty space with no one else to hear.

God wanted him, so God took him! From the bottom of my heart, I yearn to have my son Patrick back with me. Patrick was my son, my mate, so close and I loved him so deeply, I am cut and my soul is slashed to the core, I miss him so much.

So, me and my brother Martin had a bond, a bond that could not be broken, brought about by the death of our own dear sons. I remember getting back to Manchester after about twelve months away with my Roseanne and my brother Martin had become almost alcoholic. He became an extremely heavy drinker for a good few years as a result of the death of his son.

During the years following the accident, we both became closer and closer as we understood each other's pain in full. Many years later Theresa died, his wife, my dear sister-in-law. She was not at all like a sister-in-law but so much more, like a true sister. We used to have such fun winding each other up for the craic. Always with a sparkle in her eyes, mischief, and fun she was!

When she died, I was doing a half marathon and our Martin was cheering me on. We had just gone for a drink after the run and we got a call from the hospital to get there as quick as we could. She had taken a turn for the worse and suddenly she died and was gone. None of us could believe it and it affected my dear Roseanne in a very bad way, along with our Martin.

Roseanne was back in a different world again, back into a world of pain and anguish at losing her dear sister who was also like my very own sister. Remember, we, all four of us, were married at the same time, we did everything together and suddenly she was gone. A massive, gaping void opened up again and it was like Roseanne had disappeared into it, removed from us, from me, altogether. Oh, she was with us in person, but not in mind. It was like she was gone from her body, totally disconnected and not there. I remember thinking she was lost to me for good this time. Thinking, I am in trouble now. I did not know how to help her get through this tragedy and come back to me again. It had been such a long journey of recovery after Patrick's death that I thought this time we had lost her for good and I felt useless, not knowing how to help her.

Theresa's funeral was so sad it was unbelievable, my brother Martin and all the family were gathered at the graveside and he sang a song for her: "*If I could turn back time… If I could find a way….*" It was stunning, so very loving and full of emotion; everyone in the graveyard was crying. I thought to myself how brave that was of him, how much bottle he had to be able to do this lovely song full of love for his dear wife. All the Doherty's came to the funeral from all over the country. I was looking at Martin singing, like you might watch a new-born baby, my eyes were super glued to him, while he finished his song.

Now, our Martin is like his Daddy, Old Quinn God bless him, he is very old-fashioned in a good way. He would not usually let anyone see his emotions, like the Queen, no one knows what's really going on inside.

Now, I knew every emotion he had got and I was watching him closely. I walked up to him and said very quietly, "Are you all right?"

"Ah Paddy, get me the fuck out of here, get me the fuck out!" he whispered under his breath.

I took him and put him in the car along with our Dudlow and we swiftly left the graveyard. Not much later, we found ourselves in a pub in Winslow, in the middle of nowhere.

We sat down and Martin says, "I need a pint badly," so I swiftly got him a drink and he quickly had two more to help take the stress away.

Eventually I said to Martin, "We need to get to the other pub where all the people attending the funeral are meeting, in North Wales."

"Yeah," he said, "I'm all right now Paddy, I feel a bit calmer after that."

We got to the pub where the wake was, I got drinks for us all and we sat outside in the sun because it was a very hot day. We sat there for about an hour and found ourselves surrounded by family for the rest of the day celebrating the life of my dear Martin's wife.

For the following twelve months, I simply did not leave Martin's side. Every single day he would want to go down the pub and I would go along with him to keep him company, so as not to be alone with his sorrow. I used to get his clothes washed, I would iron his trousers and shirt myself, every second day I found myself doing his clothing for him, to keep him looking right and proper.

The time went by and he had a fabulous headstone made for Theresa's grave, just simple and nice honouring her name. It wasn't a big monument, a headstone is not going to get you into Heaven, it's not what it looks like or how big it is, you could put a shoe over and you would have more chance of getting into Heaven than a palace over a grave.
So, we celebrate the life of someone after twelve months at the headstone blessing, the crowd was fantastic and Martin was so proud to see all the people celebrating with us, we

went to a nearby pub and it was full of people remembering Theresa's life with joy.

Afterwards that evening we went to a pub nearer home, me, Martin and Dudlow. The three brothers or as we used to say, 'The Three Amigos'. After a little while we found ourselves laughing, joking again and enjoying life.

I said, "Martin, I've got news to tell you. After tomorrow I am not drinking everyday with you!" I said it in a fun way, "Because I can't keep it up! I've done my twelve months with ya and that's it I am gone!"

He started laughing and our Dudlow says, "Am I glad to hear that, our Paddy, 'cos I can't keep up with this either!" he said laughing his boots off.

We found ourselves laughing and joking, having fun and enjoying life for the first time in so many years. It was unreal, fun and joyous to see the smile on our Martin's face, Dudlow having fun and feeling the muscles in my stomach ache from so much laughing. We felt joy in our hearts at last.

Our Martin said, "I am finished with it myself!"

"Thank God!" I said, with a big fat smile on my face.

After that time, it was like something happened and Martin finally slowed down on the drink, finding himself again, just as I had. Everything was finally normal again and one day Martin came over to our chalet, carrying a ton of shirts over one arm.

"Can you just iron these for me our Paddy?"

"I will on my bollocks!" I said, handing them back and hearing myself roaring with laughter at last.

"I told you, I have done my twelve months and I am done! Ya can iron them yourselves now ya bollocks!"

He roared back with laughter too, a huge smile all over his face. We know each other's moves, each other's thoughts, almost before the other one has thought it, it's like a connection that can never be lost. I know if he is upset and he knows exactly the same for me.

It's part of our custom to look after your brother, sister or family in that way for twelve months following a close one's death.

Sometimes he will say to me, "Now Paddy, did you take a tablet?"

I think to myself, he knows I haven't. I am not ashamed to say, I take a tablet to keep my mood good, an antidepressant these days and if I fail to take them it shows. If I fail to take them, he knows and quite rightly, he won't let me slip because he loves me.

Now, my Daddy – he said to me, "Do not cry at my funeral," he said, "I want you singing, dancing and I want you happy!" We did that for him, we were all singing, dancing and happy. It's what he wanted and it's what we gave him. But even so, by the minute it was over and I was driving down the motorway, I could not stop crying. There was no one there to see and I could cry any way I wanted to. It was when I was with the other people I could not cry.

I miss my brother Charlie. I loved him more than anything in the world, I never thought it was possible to love a brother the way I loved our Charlie. When Charlie passed away, I fell more in love with my other brother Francie. He took Charlie's place in many ways.

Me and our Francie used to have real-close, personal talks. Whenever me and my father fell out, you would see our Francie trying to be the go between with us. Then suddenly our Francie died, gone, suddenly, like a rain drop hitting the ocean and merging with the sea. When that happened a part of me died with him. Genuinely a part of me went when he did. He had cystic fibrosis. God rest his soul; I loved him and miss him so much. He was like a social worker for me, now that might sound a bit silly a big man like me, but it's the truth. He was so intelligent, sensitive and clever in so many ways. You could tell him anything and he would take it to his grave without a soul ever knowing. I used to tell him everything and anything, knowing it would sit with him and go no further, perfect trust. I had one of the biggest heartbreaks in my life when he died. He was so special to me; it was just unbelievable. I loved him because he was a part of me. With the mixed-up life I had, mixed up world I felt I was living in, there are no words to describe the love I felt for this man. No heart can express how deep that love was. Reaching out and beyond the stars and back for this man would never have been enough! GOD REST HIS SOUL!

I remember at my Sister Mary son's funeral, Mikey Connors, another great chap as a fighter, he could sing like a dream, a wonderful dancer, a very well to do boy with a big stud farm, good looking and everyone wanted a bit of him, like Father

Christmas! He had two beautiful children, Michael and Mary. He died driving a horse and cart when a car hit him and killed them both sadly. He was an incredibly wealthy man in so many ways. He did loads for charity; it was just fantastic how hard he worked. He is greatly missed, along with my father and the Old Queen, as I have already said, she died when she had given up, when her heart was broken, following my father's death. She waited until she had placed the headstone on my father's grave and the following day she passed.

Christie Joyce was like a father figure to me, a strong, good man. It was always a great honour just to go up to him and shake his hand or give him a kiss and losing him to the Corona Virus was so painful to me, it was like losing my own father all over again. His wife, Winnie, was a pure lady and the two of them were tailor made for each other, it was like putting a glove on a hand – they fit each other just so snugly. They are resting together now. I feel so very sorry for the family. God rest the Oxford Joyces, as they were known, and I have known them since I was a small child. Sixty-one years – how the time has floated on by like a whisper on the wind.

Anyone past fifty reading this will understand this because when you reach that age, it seems you are always going to funerals with only the occasional wedding. Past fifty, it comes as a shock because you don't feel at all old but sadly now, it's funeral after funeral after funeral.

## *Vices*

I can genuinely say, I have never sold a drug in my life, on my son Patrick's grave, I can swear this. I took drugs, when my son died, I took everything to try and get away from the pain, I simply did not care and I wanted my life gone. I remember at that time, in the bleakest of times, I went down in weight to about seven stones. I got my life back in time and I have never taken a drug since, it's the very last thing I would ever want to do. The last time I ever took drugs was over ten years ago now. When I kicked them, I left Manchester, a new start, I had just finished *Celebrity Big Brother*. It was about this time or just before then that I used to do a great deal of 'Charlie', cocaine.

I will never ever again go anywhere near anything like that for as long as I live. Anyone who is doing that stuff is chasing nothing, they are on the road to nowhere and are complete fools. The thing about those sorts of drugs is that they change your mindset and you think you're going to get this and that and be super rich, super liked, SUPERHUMAN! IT'S ALL NONSENSE!

No matter who you are, in the end you come back to the real world, except your problems seem ten times worse than before. I know and have met a lot of drug dealers in my time, big time drug dealers and all of them have gone the same way. They have nothing left at all, not a pot to piss in as they might say. They all had the money, they had the clothes, the swag, the girls, the sporty cars, the big houses, you name it they had it and now they have NOTHING!

There were many times I was asked to put my name to certain drug deals and things of that type, but I refused, always. People, dealers, would say to me, just put your name to this that or the other, you'll make a fortune. We will pay you fifty percent of the deal.

"No, no – NO!" I would fire straight back, "I want nothing to do with it." They got the message in time and left me alone, but it did take time.

I am pleased to say I always earned my money and never sold a drug in my life, nor did I ever give anyone a drug to get them hooked. I am so pleased to be able to say that I never sold a drug to a soul. I always believed that if I was to introduce someone to a person who sold drugs, or if I gave anyone drugs, then I would be just as bad a person as the dealer themselves. I always felt it was for the dealers to do what they wished but ultimately, they had to answer to their own conscience for whatever they did. It did not feel right for me to be telling them how to live their lives. I never would have been able to live with myself if I had done such a thing. I genuinely would not have been able to live with myself. I know that when I go to my God, he will know that I am telling the truth and ultimately, that's what matters to me.

I got into gambling though and that was a bad, terrible thing for me and my family. It was like a drug for me the gambling was. I would find myself in a casino and my name would be well known. I know that you really cannot mess with these people because they are beyond gangsters, they are the real gangsters of gangsters. When you get gripped like I was, before you know it, you are losing hundreds of thousands of pounds. Then suddenly you don't have the money anymore, it's all gone.

I remember my lovely Roseanne asking me one day, "Paddy, what are you doing with your money?" She was so harmless, it's why we love each other so much, we do, I am her and she is me.

## *Depression*

Not just me, but Roseanne too. She is in a bad place at the moment. She's in the middle of a breakdown, she can go to bed and stay there for a week or ten days without coming out of the bedroom. When she is like this, it is very hard for her and for me, to see her like that too. Your home just feels empty and lifeless. We have a beautiful home, fit for a queen, but it feels empty, you need your wife with you, to go up to the shops together or go to the local pub, bar or restaurant for a bite to eat. None of that is happening at the moment. She is not selfish, far from it, she's just bad with her nerves. I have been very bad with my nerves so I understand, it can happen to anyone of us.

When everything snowballed for me and I was working what felt like twenty-four hours a day, seven days a week, it felt like I was working for nothing or very little. I wasn't being paid right, I knew I was losing major money, it was going somewhere but I was not seeing a lot of it. The main trouble was that my life was really mixed up at that time, all the hype after *Celebrity Big Brother*, the pressure of all the television appearances, where I didn't know whether they were genuinely interested in me, or I was the butt of their jokes and actually they were mocking me. Followed and hounded by the media, just waiting for me to 'eff' it all up. Then the Inland Revenue came after me, investigating my tax situation which should have been dealt with by my manager, it was just horrendous. When I finally got the tax situation sorted out, I was left with nothing, no money and very little income. It didn't bankrupt me, but I still owe them money and I am still paying them back now, one bit at a time, it feels like it will never end, it never leaves you! So, I didn't realise at the time that I was slowly breaking down, falling into a depression all the while, everything I had worked for was just washing away. This all happened over a twelve-to-fourteen-month period and for me to finally figure out what was happening to me and why I was feeling the way I was.

Over time my depression got really bad. I didn't know that I was severely depressed. No one really appreciates that situation and I certainly didn't. It creeps up on you like a twisted boa constrictor, slowly suffocating you, until one day you find that you don't want to wake up anymore.
I was at the stage of really not wanting to wake up and I knew I had to do something about it, so one day I plucked up the

courage to go to the doctor. He asked me a whole load of questions after which he looked me in the eye and told me, with that cool assuredness and matter-of-factness that doctors have, that I needed help. He recommended a good female psychiatrist who he thought would be able to help me.

I didn't really know where else to turn, but I trusted the doctor and took his advice. I soon found myself in Wythenshawe, Manchester, in a small cubicle facing a woman who was about to embark with me on a journey of understanding, expression of feelings, exploration of causes and of course, help.

My psychiatrist, a professor of psychology, was a real lady, with kind eyes and strong features. I kept forgetting her name and after I'd been going for a few weeks I had to apologise to her for not remembering it. She looked at me with real care in her eyes and told me not to worry, to just think of a particular season when I saw her – winter – she made it so easy and relaxed for me, no mockery or disappointment, just genuine care.

At the beginning I had to see her three times a week but after a while, when we were making good progress, it reduced to once a week, and then every fortnight. This was a really long journey and it took two years for me to get back to a degree of what you or I would call normal.

At first, we were just getting to know each other, introducing myself to this exploration of my mind and deepest thoughts. What I didn't realise, was how smart she was, how she teased everything out of me, and I mean everything.

I'm not ashamed to admit it, but I was suicidal at that time and this felt like my last chance. The depression had gripped me so badly that I just could not see any way out. There are of course hundreds of thousands of people suffering the same kind of feelings of unhappiness or hopelessness, low self-esteem or finding no pleasure in things they usually enjoy. Their situations, triggers and solutions might be different, but the feelings and the degree to which they feel them (never mind the way it can make you physically feel too) are the same. However, at the time you think there is no one else who could possibly be in such a place but yourself.

Eventually I started to open up to her and slowly began to divulge my real problems, how bad things were, how I really felt inside and how my life had been turned upside down when I reached the dubious status of 'celebrity'. How isolating it was and how I felt swamped by the television shows and their demands of me. It felt crazy, with people dragging me here, there and everywhere, asking me to do this, that and the other and how, wherever I turned it felt as if people were wanting to fight me, just to have a go at me, so they too could get in the newspapers.

I remember telling my psychiatrist about the time Roseanne and I were lucky enough to go away to Turkey with our friends Tracy and Peter, just for a break to get away from things. They had a beautiful, extensive villa in Turkey, it was absolutely stunning, so quiet and relaxing, no one on the doorstep, privacy and tranquility, Heaven. There we were over two thousand miles away from home, leaving behind all the worries, people and feelings of being trapped, strolling down to the local village paper shop on the first morning, only to see myself splashed all over the Turkish magazines. I showed the publications to Roseanne, my voice was quivering and I felt really shaky. I just genuinely could not handle the pressure.

They always say, 'there's a light at the end of the tunnel' but when you're depressed you put a mask on, to make others think that you're great and that there's nothing wrong at all, or that you've never been happier. Like Turkey, the truth is far from it.

Seeing this unexpected publicity in the papers, in another country, really unsettled me and I found myself walking alone for miles until I discovered a small, isolated church, right in the middle of a mountain. It was so quiet and peaceful, nobody around, I could just sit and talk to God. I absolutely loved going there because I was on my own, I could talk to God in the way I wanted to talk to God. I don't want people thinking I'm this great, devout Christian, but I'm a bit better now than I used to be. I try my best and here, in this tiny place of worship miles from anywhere, I found some solace with my God.

I was telling the psychiatrist all of this and she asked me how many times I'd tried to kill myself. I did not see that question coming and asked her what she meant.

"Well," she said, "you clearly wanted to escape the world." She had a really lovely way of putting it. I found myself telling her honestly, confessing for the first time, how I had taken three or four overdoses. I told her one night my wife was in bed beside me and I remember getting up out of bed, taking myself to the other bedroom and taking handfuls of tablets – every single tablet I could find in the house. As I was about to drift off to sleep I was asking God to forgive me and have mercy on my soul.

"Please, please have mercy on my soul."

While I was saying these things to God, lying on the bed staring up at the ceiling, I felt myself slowly slipping away, thinking then, that I was probably about to die. I told her how I just wanted to die, desperate for the relief, the release from the never-ending agony. I wanted to get away, escape from everyone and everything. I didn't care for my wife, my children, my grandchildren or anyone – I just had this black void. Nobody could possibly imagine what I was going through, what pain I was in, I just needed it to stop.

I slept for two days solid, eventually waking up not knowing where I was, dizzy as hell. It took me a long time to realise where I was and that I was not dead after all. I then became really angry with myself for having taken all these tablets and being sick for two days.

The psychiatrist looked at me and quietly asked me what I did next. I told her how I stayed in bed staring at the ceiling and that Roseanne didn't have a clue what I'd done, no one had the slightest inkling. I had kept it as my little secret. I told her that you just do that when you're depressed – you keep all your depression and thoughts to yourself. I felt so desperately alone.

I didn't tell my woman anything about this because I knew she wasn't well enough to handle it herself. I really did feel I had no one to talk to. Depression is a really dark place. It's pitch black, surrounding you and dragging you down into a black hole of nothingness. I already know that feeling because it had happened to me before, when I was shot in the head on my own doorstep.

Here's what happened. I remember the day I got shot by my front door at the chalet. My little man Martin-Tom was with me. I got shot at my front door and I'll never forget that day until the day I die (again).

This chap, this dummy with a gun, pulls up in a van.

"Paddy Doherty, I'm here to shoot ya!" He shouted over at me.

"You couldn't shoot no one! I'm going to take that gun and shove it back up your rear end!" I said back to him.

He was shaking like a leaf, with the gun in his hand. We had a bit of an argument between each other, I told my Martin-Tom to go inside the chalet out of the way.

I wanted to hit this fella so bad, but I didn't want my son to see it all happening and as I turned back to the shooter, from telling my Martin-Tom to go inside, he shot me!

I really thought at times, I really, really thought I was indestructible, because I've had a gun put to me so many times, it was nothing to me. A bullet, a gun, a machete, they were nothing to me, I'd walk straight into it, because I feared nothing, feared no one, I only fear God all right.

He'd shot me while I had my back to him and it hit me in the back of the head. I went down face first, I fell, that was it! The bullet must have come out of my forehead.

I remember, I was dead, on the stairs, on the ground, dead, on my face on the ground. Martin-Tom was forced to run inside to get his Mummy. Roseanne told me all this afterwards. Martin-Tom had run into the house screaming! "Mammy, Dad...Daddy's been shot!"

She came running out and she rolled me over, she's there on her knees with my head on her thighs and she's roaring and crying, she's hitting me in the chest.

"Paddy, Paddy, wake up, wake up!"

I swear on my life, on my life, on my lovely son's life and my lovely Roseanne's life, I see myself looking down at Roseanne while she's beating my chest.

"Wake up Paddy, wake up, wake up," she's crying and I was bleeding, I was in a bad way, like, it was just weird. I'm looking at myself on the ground and looking at my own body – it was an out of body experience – I've heard people tell of it, but never for one minute thought there was any truth in it. I'd never experienced it before in my life and I'm saying to myself, 'I'm done, I'm really done for this time.'

"Roseanne, cover yourself up woman," I was saying. It's funny when I think of it now, but I was looking down at us on the floor, in the entrance to our home and all I could see was Roseanne in her nightgown and bra. We're old-fashioned people and I was more worried that her chest was showing.

The next minute it starts going darker and darker, it was going like black is black, but it was so dark, you couldn't even see your hand in front of your face, I've never experienced a darkness like that before in my life. It was frightening, that's how dark it was. It was like a shutter coming down, down, down. I knew I was dead, in my head I was saying exactly this, 'I'm dead, I must be dead.' When I knew this, the next thing that popped into my thoughts was, 'Please, my God forgive me, forgive everything I've ever done on this Earth. Please, my God, have mercy on me, please have mercy on me and look out for my children. Please, have mercy on me, when I come for my judgement, have mercy on me, please.' I didn't say, 'Let me live, let me live,' I just wanted mercy from my God because I knew I was dying.

I swear on my life, the next minute, I woke up in the back of an ambulance being given the electric shock, '*WHOOMPH, WHOOMPH.*' They brought me back to life. I knew no one saved me, no one saved me that time, God gave me my life back, my God gave me back my life.

I was in the hospital, in intensive care and it was so creepy, I'll never forget it. They told me what they'd done. I came out of intensive care, then out of the hospital and about two months after, I got back into the gym, like none of it ever happened. Then I'd go up the road, running, and suddenly I'd start to feel paranoid. Was someone waiting for me? Were they going to jump out at me? Is someone waiting to jump out and shoot me, finish me off? Then it just got ridiculous. I was paranoid of everyone and everything, but to look at me you'd think there was nothing wrong with me. But I knew there was something wrong with me and so did Roseanne. She told me to go to the doctors. So, I did.

I was driving to the doctors in the car and looking in the rear-view mirror. I felt like someone was in the car behind me, following me, after me. I told the doctor everything and he said, "You've had a mental break, Mr Doherty, a bad breakdown." So, he gave me 'nerve' tablets.

There were a few times that I wanted to do harm to myself. You see this face, my face and you think nothing's bothering me, everyone thinks you're 'happy-go-lucky' but you're not.

So, I'm taking these tablets, banging them down my neck just to keep right.

To have a nervous breakdown, there are no words for it. It's like a woman going into labour, there are no words for it, she's says the pain is horrendous but she can't describe it to me, well, that's what a breakdown is like, you can't describe it. It gives you no warning, no advice, no idea of what's going to come on now.

I'm still on the tablets, I'll be on them till the day I die, I suppose. If I take a tablet now, I can talk right, I can talk all day, I can go and have a drink, I can do whatever I want and I'm lovely and calm. Three times I've tried to come off them, no, I tell a lie, about a hundred times I've tried to come off them and I'm okay for one, two, three days tops but then all of a sudden 'POOF!' my brain just falls in, I fall in.

It's a bad, bad experience, and I mean it, to whoever reads this book, if you ever start falling into a depression, when everything feels like it's closing in on top of you, and you're ready to explode, like when you open a can of coke up and you get that spurt of gas, '*PsssssssssssssssssschT*', well that's

230

what's built up inside of you, that's what depression is like, and you need to open it to release it. It gives you no warning, it just explodes! And I don't care who you are or what you are, go see a doctor or just tell someone, someone who is close to you, someone you trust, that won't just try to make you laugh and think that that's solved your depression and please take my advice, or advice off them, because I wouldn't wish it on anyone in the world.

I then told my psychiatrist about another time I attempted suicide. It was about two o'clock in the morning, it was a cold, dark night and I went outside, walked to the main road, not far from my house at all. I wasn't even thinking straight. I waited and watched, then I saw the headlights and a car driving towards me. When it was close enough, I just jumped, threw myself in front of the car. The nearside of the car hit me and I flew into the air and bounced back onto the kerb. The poor driver slammed on his brakes and jumped out of his car, frightened to death, apologising profusely and asking if I was all right. He was really shaken up and he wanted to call the police and an ambulance and he just kept on apologising. I said, "No, no, just leave me alone. It's okay I'm fine, I'm fine, I'm really sorry!" I picked myself up from the ground and walked away with blood dripping from my head.

I carried on walking around aimlessly until four or five in the morning. All the time I was walking around I was looking at the ground, not hearing anything going on, only hearing my own internal voice, contradicting me, making me think one minute that I was a failure, I failed to die, I failed my family, they would have to put up with me being miserable and unresponsive one minute, then manically happy the next. The next minute thinking, talking to myself in my head, 'Paddy, you idiot, you bastard! Look at what you done to that driver, you could have ruined that poor man's life.' I apologised to God and I was sorry, because I could sympathise with how that man felt. I knew because my son, my nephew and my nephew's first cousin were all killed in a car accident; the lorry driver who accidentally killed them never got over it. I said to myself, 'look what you have done,' and I knew I would never do that again. To hurt someone like that is wrong. It's not that the depression makes you evil, wanting to hurt anyone else or blame anyone else. You just find that you don't even consider other people, it doesn't enter your head that you can have a massive impact on others with your actions when you are so depressed with your life and you just don't know what you are doing any more and you don't care either at the time.

I finally found myself back at home. I climbed back into bed and eventually fell asleep. Roseanne had no idea that I'd been out of bed, never mind what I had attempted in the dead of night or that I ruined someone else's life in the process and was now riddled with guilt and feelings of unworthiness.

The next day I got up, quite bruised and a bit battered but I didn't tell my woman, my sons or my daughter. I told no one. But I made a promise to myself that I would never do that again, however many times I felt like I wanted to.

Thankfully, I am seeing the light at the end of the tunnel, finally, and I am coming out of the depression and anxiety now. Having gone through such turmoil myself and seeing people like Tyson Fury, who is such a great, tough man amongst the Traveller community, seeing that he was able to open up and share his own battles with problems like these, fills me with pride and deep respect for him, having the courage to do that. In part he helped me overcome the stereotypical view I had of myself: *Big Men Don't Cry*, real men don't get depressed or anxious, in our culture we don't show any weaknesses – we have no weaknesses! We are real men, tough, hard, protective, loving, feared and respected. Not wallowing in self-pity, suffering with the invisible disease that no one wants to acknowledge or talk about. It's just not done. I am a MAN. I thank God for the wisdom to break down my own barriers and to seek the help I so desperately needed.

When you're depressed you can't always see it, other people don't see it either. Why? Because a lot of people hide it, they put on a mask of happiness and hide it so well it's totally believable. They look stunning, have all the visible trappings of wealth; fantastic jewellery, clothes, cars, houses, everything. The outside looks amazing and you would think that such a person is the happiest in the world. But no one knows what's going on inside their heads, they could be severely depressed, their family messed up, like I was messed up.

I simply felt I had no reason to live, no reason to live at all, I thought. That's the truth. I am not suicidal now and I hope and pray that it will never happen again but you can never be sure. Naturally, everyone in the world has bad days, it's normal to worry about silly, inconsequential things but they don't feel silly at the time.

My psychiatrist, my saviour, got so much information out of me and of course, everything stays totally confidential, she would never tell a soul anything we talk about, she never shares anything with anybody. By the way, and I hope she won't mind me saying so, she also happens to be a very attractive woman and was always immaculately dressed. I have always enjoyed looking at people and noticing how they dress and she clearly had very good taste and cared about how she presented herself. Clothes tell me a lot about people. I always kept my appointments and never missed a single one and after each session I would always feel great for several days. I felt a great sense of relief, as though the weight of my burdens had been lifted from me and dumped somewhere else.

I found these sessions so beneficial that I continued the therapy for three years. I was also told that, if I felt it necessary, if I felt particularly bad and desperate to get away, I could always stay overnight in the psychiatric ward.

Miss Winter got a lot out of me and until the day God takes me off this Earth, I will never forget her. She will always have a place in my heart and also in my wife's heart. I always talk about her, even my sons know about her – they don't know the details of our conversations but they know about her. Thinking about her now, I realise I still don't even know her first name, even after seeing her for three years, such was the nature of the professional relationship. I truly believe she saved my life. My family has no idea how much I wanted to kill myself at that time. Thanks to Miss Winter I have learned to come to terms with and live with things now.

She taught me specific techniques to help me cope with certain difficulties in life. If someone does something to you to forget about it, and don't let them into your head. She taught me how to do that some of the time. As it says in the *Bible*, you have to forgive and if you don't forgive you cannot enter the Kingdom of Heaven.

Once you get this problem you never escape from it, I am not ashamed to say that I take a tablet every day of my life, I can talk normal, see people normal, go for a drink and chat normal, have a laugh and a joke. It helps just enough to stop

236

me thinking about the bad things inside my head. The medication prescribed by the doc have given me the element of peace that I crave in my life, they calm me down just enough to live in this world, so I would say to anyone if you are struggling with mental health issues go to the doctor, don't be ashamed and get help.

I used to run away from it, deny it and hid it all the time and my God did I suffer as a result. Miss Winter, my psychiatrist was the saving grace for me, she has helped me so much, words are not enough to thank her. I still see her even now, to top up 'my better me' so to speak.

It was an honour and an expression of her trust in me when she introduced her family to me. Just lovely, the best thing in the world to me because she was such a lady of pedigree, she did not have to do it but it meant so much to be trusted by someone like her. We'd meet, have a chat, I offload, drink a glass of orange juice; she is such a good lady to me with lovely daughters and a brother called Chris. The whole family are just great. I have been privileged to meet them all, her mother and sister, all of them just great people to me.

I am so blessed, because whenever I am suffering, which can happen at any time, I can pick up the phone and give her a call and within a few minutes of talking with her she helps me get some sanity back, helps me calm myself and understand what is really going on. No one really knows about depression until you are in it. These brilliant people give one of the greatest gifts anyone can give. They are trained to find avenues into peace, to understanding of your own thoughts and bring some order into a disrupted mind.

I am very grateful that most days now I am okay and understand what's going on. More good days than bad days.

So, I give thanks to Miss Winter for saving my life. I am now sixty-one and I can't see myself ever trying to kill myself again thanks to her and my God. I truly think God has a plan for me in the future. Miss Winter also went to see Roseanne and I want to thank her so much for all the great help she has given me.

But life goes on and what I really, really enjoy are the feelings of joy and happiness I feel when I pass someone and call out, "Good Morning!" It lifts me and sets me up for the day, walking by with a smile on my face. So, I had a bad fall, a bad breakdown, my nerves got the better of me but I'm working on it every day of my life from now until the end with as much positivity as I can muster each day. When you suffer with depression you always have ups and downs and depression will never leave you alone, it sits on your shoulder waiting to bite you in the neck at any time, it is with you for life.

It's unbelievable when I think of it all now, I'm almost a completely different person. Life, on the whole, since *Celebrity Big Brother* has been very good to me. I don't want to die now of course but if I did I would accept it.

So, they say 'every cloud has a silver lining' don't they? Well, not for me it seems! Just when I'm getting on top of my depression and feeling more in control every day, I started with the most excruciating pain you can imagine. I was diagnosed with prostate cancer. Bad news. When will this ever end?

## *Cancer*

Then to top it all I was told some bad news – in 2018, I was diagnosed with prostate cancer.

When you think you're going to die with cancer, a penny drops and your life changes dramatically and completely. I wanted something to live for, I needed something to live for.

People think I have a great life, but I haven't got a great life all the time, I've got a sad life sometimes.

It all started when I noticed blood in my pee when I went to the toilet. I ignored it because I was embarrassed to go to the doctor with it. I'm not embarrassed to talk about it now though, because, if my experiences help just one man or many men to understand the agony of it, the signs to watch out for and as a result they seek early treatment, then my job is done.

It started to get really difficult to go to the toilet. Besides the blood, the pain started and it got progressively worse. Even when you don't fear anyone and you are used to taking and feeling pain, you think nothing can hurt you anymore, but this pain was so bad that it felt like razor blades were coming out and it made my eyes roll up into the back of my head and wished I was dead at times.

You try to pee and you squeeze so hard for only a tiny drop to come out. You keep trying and the pain is so bad you can hear the screaming before you realise it's your own screams you can hear and you have to hold onto something because any minute you might pass out.

Whenever I was away from the house, you know out with our Martin, in the pub or somewhere else very public, I always had to go into the cubicle and not use the urinals for embarrassment and to try and hide the evidence and pain. My brother Martin would stand guard and say to people wanting to do the 'other' that there was someone in there.

I imagine the pain is like a woman in labour or maybe worse, like having surgery without anaesthetic. Sometimes, some days the urine was nothing but blood, but I got to the point where I just could not go without this almighty pain. I'd push, push and push more, but nothing was coming out! At that time and in that moment while I was in so much pain, I just wished I was dead. I wasn't really that keen on dying, I didn't truly want to die but I could not live with the constant pain, the blood and the fear.

I would not have wished this pain on any human being it was just so evil. You would have to be so full of bitterness to wish this type of pain on anyone. I knelt down before my God and asked for forgiveness for all my evil thoughts.

It got harder and harder to hide the truth of it from my Roseanne. She could hear me moaning in the toilet. At first, she'd be asking, "Are you okay, Paddy?" As per usual, I would deny anything was wrong and tell her I was okay, that I was just busting for a pee and it was relief that made me moan. How long can you keep that up for? Not long, I tell you. It might just have been an infection or something, but the pain continued to get worse and the blood just kept on coming.

I couldn't hide the pain from Roseanne, she could still hear me moaning in the toilet. She'd call out to me, "Paddy what's wrong?" I'd tell her to leave me alone, nothing was wrong.

This went on for about three to four months and as the pain worsened and the amount of blood increased, even while the amount of pee reduced, I found myself getting more and more angry, looking to the bottle, using the booze to try and blot it out. There was no hiding it from her any longer and I had to tell her what was going on. Roseanne made me go to see the doctor. The pain was excruciating.

I made the appointment and asked for a male doctor, because it's embarrassing to get your tackle out in front of a lady that's not your wife, plus I had an idea they would want to examine them! No way was that going to happen with a woman doctor!

So, I went to the doctors, he asked me questions and I described the blood, the pain and the lack of flow, how I had to push and squeeze every drop out, how it was so painful I had to stifle the screams and how it made me feel like I was going to pass out. He explained that a lot of men my age, start to have problems with their prostate gland and that as you get older, sometimes it can swell up and when it does that, then it can cause problems with peeing because it squashes the tube that the pee comes through from your bladder. He said he needed to examine me and I thought 'okay, I knew this might happen and he'd need to look at my tackle,' so I stood and dropped my pants.

The doctor said to me, "No, Mr Doherty, I need you to get on the table, with your back towards me, and I want you to bring your knees up to your chest, please."

I was thinking, 'why does he want me to do that?' So, I asked him and he explained that the only way he could examine my prostrate was to do a rectal examination. 'Oh My God,' I thought, 'that's not natural,' but I didn't really have any options at that point, did I? I got up on to the table like he asked and braced myself.

He said to me, "Just relax Mr Doherty, this will be much easier and quicker if you relax. You will feel something cold, which is just a lubricant to make it easier, then you will feel pressure. Are you ready?"

In my head I'm like, 'NO, AM I FUCK READY,' but then I said, "Yes, go ahead."

I've never been so embarrassed in my life. I know it only took less than a minute, but it felt like ten! When he was finished, the doctor said to me, "Okay, Mr Doherty, all done. You can get dressed now." I had never felt relief like it, to be able to get dressed again and cover up.

I expected him to explain what he'd found, but he didn't, well not straight away, he asked me more questions, like, how long had it been going on for, why I hadn't gone to the doctors when it first started to happen, whether my sex life had been affected by it and a load of other stuff. I'm thinking, 'what's that got to do with anything?' Anyway, I answered his questions and revealed that I'd been suffering for months without telling anyone except my brother and that it was my woman who made me come to the doctors.

The doctor told me the gland was definitely enlarged and that because of all the symptoms and the length of time I had left it without getting it checked, he couldn't rule out the possibility that I might have prostate cancer, but that I would need further tests to confirm it one way or another. I was speechless, numb, scared, angry all at the same time. 'Fuck, I'm gonna die, again,' was going through my mind. 'How many times is this shit gonna happen to me? Why is God punishing me like this?'

"Mr Doherty," the doctor said, bringing me out of my inner thinking, "I'm going to give you a form to take to the hospital. You need to go straight there, today. They will do the extra tests and when we get the results, we can decide on a treatment plan, okay?"

I said, "Doctor, be honest with me, am I going to live or am I going to die?"

He said, "Honestly, this has been going on far too long. If you do have cancer, provided it hasn't spread, the treatment and prognosis is usually very good. Even if it has spread, there are other options we can consider that may save your life or prolong it, but we'll talk about that once the tests have confirmed the severity. You will likely need surgery and possibly chemotherapy. Go get the tests done and we'll take it from there, okay?"

I went straight to the hospital like the doctor said, but I had no idea where to go in the hospital. I waited by the main reception until only a man was at the desk and I showed him the form asking where I needed to go and he gave me directions. I eventually found where he told me to go and took a seat in this little office.

Someone came in and said, "You have to go to another part of the hospital to have your prostate checked."

By this point I'm totally confused, I had no idea where they were telling me to go, or even what a prostate was.

So, they took blood to test and also did some kind of scan, I wasn't really taking it all in. I was again subjected to a rectal examination.

To cut a long story short, I was told that they used some kind of scale to measure the severity of it against, something like A, B, C and D and they told me mine was on a D.

They said, "Paddy, we've got to put you on steroids," because they weren't sure if I had the cancer or not. Apparently, they are supposed to reduce the swelling! The steroids didn't clear up the symptoms, so I asked for them to give me more, I was stubborn, it was so embarrassing, I'm a proper man me, I'm a man's man, you know? When they refused, I told them just to cut 'it' off then (and you know what I mean by 'it'!) I couldn't stand the pain anymore.

"I don't care – just take 'it' off!"

The doctor said I would need two operations, one of the doctors was a professor, and I told them that two operations were no good to me, that they should do them both in one go.

He said to me, "Do you realise how much pain you will be in after the operation?"

I said, "Well, it can't be any worse than the pain I have now, can it?"

He kept saying, "No, you don't understand…"

I kept saying back, "No, YOU don't understand!"

I asked him if he'd ever had prostate problems before and he said, "No."

So, I said, "You have no idea then, how painful this is now never mind after the operations! I have no idea how much pain a woman has when she's giving birth, but I would not wish this pain on an animal never mind a human being!"

Then he talked me through everything and said I had to sign some papers.

I was like, "What do I have to sign them for?" and he said, "So you don't come back a sue us afterwards."

I went in the hospital that morning for my operation, I hadn't told Roseanne anything about it at this point, and I was shocked when they said they thought I may have cancer in my testicles as well, it might have spread.

"When we cut you open, we'll know how far it's gone."
I was just like, "Look don't tell me the details, just do what
you have to do to make me right again." Essentially, I was
giving them permission to remove my testicles if they found
it necessary, so I had no clue whether I would have any or
not after the operation.

They took my prostate out completely, and luckily my
testicles were one hundred percent okay, which was a massive
relief. They told me everything was ok. 'Everything' is still in
working order and my woman knows that now too! A lot of
men shy away from getting this problem seen to for fear that
they won't 'function' properly after treatment.

It's funny actually, because when you go down for surgery
and they are getting you ready for the anaesthetic, they said to
me that sometimes people's teeth get damaged when they put
the breathing tube down your throat and I said jokingly,
"Forget the operation, you're not breaking my teeth!"
The anaesthetist was shocked because he thought I meant it
but in the end I agreed. Straight after though, as I was coming
round, the first thing I wanted to know was if my teeth were

okay! – the Doherty smile is more important than my member!!

I had two operations in the end, and on the final one they came and said, "Wake up, wake up," and I did.

I asked if everything was all right now and they said to me, "You're all right now, Mr Doherty, everything is lovely, you just need to take this tablet every day,"

From that day until now and every day to come, I thank you my God, my Jesus, I am okay. I was put on steroids permanently (well I think they are steroids, but I'm not one hundred percent sure, it could be a hormone tablet and I don't care as long as they keep me right) one in the morning one at night for the rest of my life I think to keep any swelling at bay. I may even get a celebratory tattoo to mark the occasion! Luckily, I am mended, it can't come back and it can't spread because it's gone.

But prostate problems if you let them go like I did, it's a bad thing. Get checked always, don't wait like I did. I would say though, to anyone who has any kind of pain downstairs, swallow your pride, none of this *King Kong* business. Go to the doctors quick sharp, it might be just a water infection or a kidney infection, no need to be embarrassed – get there!

We all die in the end and we all have to meet our maker so don't think evil thoughts, but don't help the Grim Reaper in his job either, like I nearly did.

Of course, any sort of bad news is a bad thing. There is an old saying – 'What money can fix; you haven't got a problem. What money can't fix; you have a big problem!'

The only thing that money can never, ever fix, is your health. No one can fix that, well except God and those NHS angels. In my opinion, God does miracles every day of the week, every second of every day, we just don't see it.

Well, I feel my God performed a miracle on me. So now I feel that God has left me here for a reason and I hope that I do something good with my time left. I feel like a cat with nine lives.
I hope I don't let Him down.

## Dan and Paddy's Bucket List

There's another good friend of mine called Danny, Danny Coll and we did a show in Japan called *Dan and Paddy's Bucket List*. Now, Danny is one of these… It's not that he's fragile, he's what you would call a bit of a quiet one, he doesn't like the violence or the shouting. If someone says something wrong to him or busting into him, he would say, "That's all right now, never mind, it's okay." You know what I mean? That's just the sort he is, unassuming and non-confrontational no matter where he is. He's not one of these to mouth off but he's the director and the producer of this programme that we were both in and he's a fantastic man.

So, this programme is a bucket list, you know, the things that you might do before you die and this bucket list was started in Japan, somewhere neither of us had been before. This was not just about going to places we'd never been before, but also about things we'd never done before that we had always wanted to do. We did all sorts of things too. We went up in a hot air balloon, we walked across the most bizarre and difficult to cross bridges, we travelled to the ocean where we saw whales and dolphins – what spectacular creatures they are! We had such a wonderful time with them. We went skydiving, but I couldn't do it because of my weight, which was a massive disappointment of me. We flew across the top of an active volcano and even went inside to get a closer look, but that's another story! You'll have to watch the programme to see it all, but there are a couple of things that really stood out for me that I do want to tell you about here.

One of the things we had to do for the filming was a bungee jump and this bridge was so high you could barely see the bottom. I've never seen anything like it in my life in terms of height and Danny was talking and laughing about this jump for about three days leading up to it. I can admit it now but I wouldn't at the time, I was worried to death, scared out of my head about this jump but no one would know it. I'm very good at putting a mask on so that I don't show my fear but I'm also extremely stubborn and when I am faced with real danger, I just love it, I can't resist it. I'm a bit of a devil that way! Danny kept laughing and joking about it as we got nearer to the time we were about to do the jump. I think he thought, 'Well, no one on this party seems afraid of what's about to happen, so it can't be that bad.' That was not the case at all. I have to tell you; I was absolutely panic stricken on the inside at the time. I was absolutely panic struck inside but, on the outside, I looked cool and collected.

Anyway, the morning arrived to finally do this jump and we took this long drive out, up into the mountains, getting higher and higher – I think it's the second highest bungee jump in the world. I can tell you this, if a man wants to die then this is a good way to do it! We got off the minibus and if you're ever going to Japan to do a bungee jump, make sure you do it at this place (Kyushu) there's a graveyard beside you and next to that there's a hospital that has a helicopter pad. So when you do the bungee jump if it doesn't go right they can send the helicopter down, get you to the hospital to see if they can get you better and if that doesn't work there's the church and the graveyard right next to it where you can be given last rights, with an undertaker so everything is sorted in the one place – result! What a place to do a bungee jump! Game, set and match, all done and dusted if it all goes wrong! Ha-ha!

The time comes and me and Dan are all kitted out, ready to do the bungee jump, now Danny normally has so much confidence, he fooled me and I think he fooled everybody. We all thought he was going to have no problem with this whatsoever. Now, the more confident he was, the more frightened I felt myself getting, although I wasn't going to admit it. Danny is not a big man, in fact he's a very small man and he's a bit of a fragile-looking fella to tell you the truth. He's a great chap and I really like him but if I was to bump into him, he'd be full of bruises in no time! I mean he is just very sensitive and I think he's quite fragile. To tell you the truth he's like a gentle teddy bear!

We walked along the bridge towards the jump platform and it felt like the longest walk you would ever do in your life.
"Look down there, look how high it is Paddy," Danny said to me.
"I'm not looking at anything!" I said back to him, eyes focusing forward and nowhere else. No way was I going to look down and frighten myself to death with the height of it. Anyway, we were waiting to get strapped in and Danny glances over at me again.
"Come on Paddy, have a look."
Well, I did, I peeped over the edge, and I was saying to myself, 'Oh, Mummy, Mummy, Mummy! Oh, help me get out of here!' I could not believe it and the fear crept in the whole of my body; I was shaking.

"What do you think?" Danny asked me.

"It looks great, I'm looking forward to this." I replied.

No one had a clue of what I was feeling inside and all I could think about was the bloody hospital, the helicopter and the graveyard with a headstone with my name on it! I bet you any money that accidents had happened here in the past. No doubt in my mind.

We moved to the edge of the platform, in the middle of the bridge and the man is there strapping people up. I looked across towards Danny and he's getting whiter and whiter and his legs are getting weaker, he looks like a vampire has drained all the blood out of him and this made me smile. I was to go first and the man gave me all the instructions, wires me up, plugs me in and got me ready to go. I'm standing looking right across the valley, I hadn't looked down at this point.

"I'm going to count you down and give you a little push and you just relax yourself and go with it, okay?" The man said to me.

"I ain't just going with it, If I'm going to go, I'm going to jump and dive out, like I've never done before, as if I'm diving into a big diving pool." I said back to him.

So, I'm stood at the edge and it's about to happen and one of the camera crew says,

"Wait! Wait! Wait! I just need to get another angle."

"On my life," I shouted at him, "get another angle! You feel this now! I am not standing here on the edge, looking down at these rocks staring at me that are going to bash me in, while you are looking for another angle, sausage!" I'm thinking to myself, 'I'm going to hit those any minute!'

"Five… Four… Three… Two… ONE!"

I jumped like I've never jumped before, dived right out like I was an Olympic diver and I hear myself screaming with delight! You can google it if you like it's out there for anybody to see. I was laughing, screaming and shouting with joy all the way down! What a thing to be able to get to do, just absolutely liberating.

I'm a bit of a sausage in some ways, I mean anything to do with death is really frightening, oh, don't get me wrong, I get really frightened but then when it gets to the edge and I have to do it, I can't wait and I have to do it, I just have to experience it! It's a way of living, a way of experiencing life, of being and feeling alive.

Eventually they get me back up to the top and as I'm getting back up Danny comes across.

"How do you feel Paddy?" He said to me.

"Danny, on my life, it is the bees' knees, it is fantastic!" I said.

"Oh, nice one," he said, looking whiter than white, with fear showing in his face and in his body.

"Listen, Danny, you'll do it, no problem, it's a piece of cake." I said to him.


Danny was up next. They were strapping him in and by now he was looking a bit green! He crawls towards the edge and he's holding on for dear life.

"Five... Four... Three... Two..."

"NO, NO, NO, NO!" Danny was shouting.

They stopped the countdown and they asked him if he was okay.

"Yeah, yeah, sure, I just need to get my concentration back." He told them.

"Don't worry Danny, you'll be fine, you're only gonna break your neck, Ha-ha!" I said to him, laughing my socks off.

Danny worked his way towards the edge again and he's practically crawling on his hands and knees.

"Hold on, let me get my concentration back."

He was getting closer to the edge, he looked like somebody who'd been put on the top floor of a thirty-four-story building that they'd forgotten to put the staircase in. He was peeping over the edge and was absolutely ashen with fear. It made me roar with laughter! He finally gets to the edge again and looks ready to jump (or be pushed) and so the guys start the countdown again.

"Five... Four... Three..."

"NO, NO, NO, NO!" Danny was shouting again.

They stopped the countdown again, sighing.

"I just need to get my concentration back again." Danny said.

"Danny, are you sure you're okay? I'll get you a priest, don't worry. There's a helicopter there that will come and get you if you need help. Don't worry if you need a hospital, it's right there too!" I said to Danny, doubled over laughing I was, I couldn't help myself.

He looked over at me as if to say, "If I could pay to get someone to beat you right now, I would, make no mistake about that!"

I was creased up laughing again. Poor Danny. But that was a look of pure fear and I knew that deep down, this was just one step too far for him. I really loved Danny, he is a great guy and a great friend, so I didn't want to hurt him or make him feel obligated to do it and I'm certainly not a bully, so I stopped with the craic when that happened to the poor guy. He was absolutely terrified.

To my utter shock, I see him turn to the bungee guy and say, "I'll do it again. I'll have one more go!"

"Go on Danny my boy, go on you can do it!" I said to him. I gave him the thumbs up. I have to say though, I was nearly peeing my pants it was so funny, but I was trying my best not to laugh.

"Excuse me, a minute," I said. I needed to turn away because I was about to burst trying to hold my laughter in. I bit my arm to try and stop myself from laughing and to stop Danny from see me doing it. I turned back around and I could see that he wasn't even looking my way anymore. I had the video camera on him and was filming away.

"Okay, if we're ready, let's start. I'll give you a bit longer to get your concentration. Here we go! Ten… Nine… Eight… Seven… Six… Five… Four… Three… Two…"

I'm thinking to myself, 'He's gonna actually do it. He's got past the Two… again.' But no…

"NO, NO, NO, NO, I just can't do it, I can't do it, I'm sorry." Said Danny again.

"What's wrong Danny?" I asked him.

"I just can't do it Paddy, I'm sorry, I'm beat." Danny said with a disappointed look on his face. I know I shouldn't have done this, but I was just so proud of myself for having done it, even though inside I was just as scared as Danny was (although no one knew it at the time).

"Yes! Yes! Yes!" I shouted.

Danny had managed to do the skydiving okay when I wasn't allowed to do it because I was too heavy, but he did it no problem and I thought he'd be able to do the bungee jump too. I felt like this was great news for me though, I was able to put all my eggs in the one basket to do this brilliant jump and Danny was the same with the skydiving. Fair play to you though Danny, you tried. So in the end we were equals, he did the skydiving and I did the bungee, great fun, the best.

Me and Danny were great together in *Dan and Paddy's Bucket List*. It was a great craic; we were fantastic together. We were like Laurel and Hardy; we never hated each other; we loved each other. What was great about Danny in the series, was that I could bounce off him and vice versa, he could bounce off of me.

Great fun, honest to God, like, I am obviously a hard man in many ways and Danny's… how I would describe a fragile man, very… sensitive. Yet, when he cracks the whip as a producer/director, he is fantastic, he comes out of his shell, so to speak, and he is right on his game. So much so that it shocked me to see him work like that. When I saw him tell the crew what to do and how to do it. Like the captain of a ship, straight forward, no messing and people jumped.
"Get here – get the sunlight – take it now before the opportunity goes."
This, that and the other, my, oh my, did he steer that ship home. He was simply fantastic at his game and no man could say otherwise. Danny could see what I could never see, or it didn't even enter my head.

One day he said to me, "Paddy we are going to this hotel, a very traditional Japanese hotel."
We got there and I was amazed, these lovely Japanese ladies came out and bowed to me and Danny, all dressed in

traditional old-style dress. I think they are called kimonos, pure silk with large, bold prints. They were just lovely, beautiful people and I remember this small, tiny, fragile lady comes out and she looked like a real princess and it turned out she was one! A few-hundred years ago, she would have been the queen of the region we were in. Her ancestors were kings and queens of the region and the hotel was the old family seat.

We were walking around this very old castle, now hotel, and my eye caught this traditional armoured suit. The type of suit that you always see the warriors wearing, in the Japanese films, set in history. It was a Samurai suit, just amazing, powerful, full of fire and life even as it stood in the big glass display cabinet, I could feel it calling me of old.

I said, "Lads, look at that for a damn suit of arms," I was in total awe at the beauty and ruggedness of the thing.

I called Danny over and said, "Hey, look at this Danny, how amazing is this?"

"Yes, it's certainly a handsome suit," he said,

"I have never seen nothing like it!" I said.

It was the real thing, the helmet, the body gear, everything. The whole thing just blew me away with the detail and the time it must have taken to make. It was three hundred years old and it looked brand, spanking new with the love, care and respect that the ancestors had maintained it in. The lady who owned the hotel, the princess, told me that it was one of her ancestors that had owned and wore it, possibly in battle. I could not stop thinking about this wonderful object and I could hear it calling me all the time as I got cleaned up from the days filming and went downstairs for a lovely meal. The lady came over to me as I was eating.

"Hello, Paddy," she said.

"Hi." I said back to her.

She spoke great English and it turned out that she had spent time in America many years previously.

"You talk very nice," she says to me with a delicate smile. It made me smile as well because it's the first time anyone had said that to me in my life!

"Thanks so very, very much ma'am, thanks lady, for that," I said, shaking her soft, delicate hand.

She then said to me, "We have a special day tomorrow, with many great guests and I wondered if you might honour me by wearing my great, great, great, great grandaddy's suit of armour in the cabinet?"

The penny didn't drop straight away and so I said to her, "What do you mean, armoured suit?"

She said, "You see the suit in the cabinet that you have admired in the glass case? That is my warrior king ancestor's suit and I would be deeply honoured if you would put it on for me tomorrow, to show the people how it looked when worn."

My face burned with joy and I found myself saying, "Mummy, I don't believe this! This is Christmas day come early. Are you sure ma'am?" I asked.

"Yes, of course I am," she smiled back.

"Thanks so very, very much," I said, shaking her hand in deep appreciation.

The next day, in the changing room, a man arrived with the suit. There was almost a ritual in putting the suit on and it took over an hour-and-a-half to finally do it.

At the end, it looked amazing and the last thing to go on was the helmet.

"This helmet is extremely heavy," the man dressing me said.

"No problem," I said to him, "don't worry about it."

Then he lowered it on to my head. I tell you, it felt like two and a half to three stone in weight, I could not believe how heavy it was.

"Oh, Mummy," I said, as he started to secure it to my head, "it's like I've got whiplash in my neck." I have to say, it was totally worth it. It looked just fantastic, the whole kaboodle, the detail in the suit of armour shone, the sword was something else and topped off by the helmet, I felt simply amazing!

So, I went out and met the people who were in awe of this suit. Just great to see it brought to life by a real-life warrior, my good self. What a sheer privilege this was.

Then, Danny decides to get his own back a little, after the fun I had had with him on the bungee jump.

"Ah, Paddy," he said, "just pop out here into this lovely traditional Japanese garden to do a little filming."

The heat was intense from the midday sun. He had me doing this and that, moving here and there in the sun, walking up and down like a model on a catwalk, posing in every which way possible.

We were in the middle of a heatwave, it was not hot-hot; it was like being in a blazing oven, being cooked from the inside out, like a turkey being readied for the Christmas dinner. I am inside this suit of armour and I am drowning in sweat, must have lost at least half-a-stone as he had me walking around.

"Do this, do that," said Danny, with a wry smile on his face. I am thinking, 'He is having a laugh with me here, he is having his laugh at me, getting me back.' Well, I pulled out my Samurai sword and I feign losing my shit! I ran around after him like a man possessed in this idyllic garden, the crew were splitting their sides as I am screaming at him, "I AM GOING TO KILL YA!"

Fair play to him, he was running around with laughter, not fear, as he knew I had finally twigged on that he had been having a laugh with me in the heat. We ended up having a great laugh at it. Clever man, all he had on was a tiny t-shirt and a pair of shorts, while me, like a big sausage, chased him around in this mad suit of armour. So, after the bungee jump and me taking the mickey out of him, he got his own back, great fun, what goes around comes around in the end. He got me lovely that time.

Another time, we were fishing and when you caught a fish you had to slice it and cook it. They were electric eels, as slippery as hell to catch but when we finally did catch them and manage to hold on to them, we cooked and ate them.

Later, we went to a factory where they prepared special fish that were a bit of a delicacy in Japan. One of the treats we had in store as it turned out, was to eat the fish's head. The ugliest-looking fish you have ever seen in your life. It must have been twenty inches long, with an eye as big as a skull. The challenge of this so-called delicacy was to eat the eye, liquor and all.

"Yes, of course we will eat it, no problem. Come on Danny," I said, thinking I will get you back this time.

Well, just as we get this delicacy in front of us, I said, "Oh, Danny, I have just got to go to the toilet."

I went and came back about five minutes later. I picked up my knife and fork as though I was going to start eating the ugly fish and then said I had to go again, pretending that I had the runs.

"I am truly sorry Danny," I said, "I just can't eat it, I am not well enough."

"I will have to eat it then, on my own," said Danny.

'Lovely,' I thought to myself. Next minute Danny is eating this ugly beast of a head. His face started to go as red as a blood red tomato.

"Are you enjoying it, Danny?" I asked him, tongue in cheek. This time I knew I had him. He gave me the look of all looks. If looks could knock me out, well this look would not have knocked me out, I would be in a coffin now, dead! I knew this time I was really angering him, because he had no choice out of politeness and the fact that someone had to eat it so it could be filmed.

But that was our banter; we would do that to each other for the craic, then ten to fifteen minutes later, when you have calmed down and you've had a sweet coffee or a Red Bull, we would get our sugar level up and we would be laughing and joking again. That was just the banter me and Danny had. I am not saying this because of Danny being who he is, but my woman loves him, my sons are mad about him, my Margaret thinks there is no one like him. Me – I think he is the bollocks! (Ha-ha, I am laughing of course) I am joking of course. Let me tell you what he is, this man, and I mean this, he is genuinely a brother to me with a different mother.

I really would have loved to have seen his Mummy or his Daddy, the point being, he is a lovely man, but he doesn't realise it, he is a comedian, but he is all brains and technology. He talks all posh, he would put Sally and John Bercow in a corner, the way he talks very posh, like he had been to Oxford and all that. His upbringing sounds like five-star class. If my friend Danny had a downfall, it would be that he trusted too many people, he seemed to trust everyone and thinks all people are like him, harmless.

He got into business with a certain fella and he did Danny over and I know this really broke him, in a way financially in part, but mainly his heart, destroyed him for a time. He still thinks the best of people, that all people are like him and he's only just learning that not all people are like that, now.

As far as I see it, or maybe learned from things that have happened to me, everyone has a skeleton to hide. My old man always said, "Keep your friends close, but keep your enemies beside you! If you love your enemy, you always know where they are and what they are up to!"

Danny is so open and honest that he seems to think only the best of people, he is so, so honest it is unbelievable. He reminds me of my Roseanne, he really cannot see wrong in any one and he doesn't like to see no wrong. He is incredibly diplomatic, if he had a problem, he would tell you. With the camera crew and directing and that, when he wants to open his mouth, he does know how to do it. He makes total sense. "You, over there with that light, camera here, sound, good…" this, that and the other at speed, he is just great with a crew and people, getting the best from them.

He must be a bit like Stephen Spielberg, the loveliest man in the world but when he gets behind that camera, no stopping him, a totally different man, nothing can stop him. Then, the next minute he goes back to being a gentleman, a lord, a sweet person but behind that camera, a bull terrier, the raging bull, 'when I say, "crack on, you will crack on!"' Well, that is what Danny is but never really a raging bull, but when he wants to be he is good. When I say good, it's like, he's a genius, he sees things like I would never be able to imagine, until I got to work with him. So, he is not a gentleman as we would say, my pal Danny, I mean this from the bottom of my heart, as true as my Patrick has gone to God, you're not a gentleman, you're a lord of a man, from all of my heart.

## *The Corona Virus*

I sometimes think, as perhaps you do, that I will be glad when this year is over. The Corona Virus, COVID-19, variants and all, but which year? 2019? 2020? 2021? Beyond? I guess it's something we'll have to live with now and for the rest of our lives.

How the world, not just the United Kingdom or Great Britain or whatever you want to call it, how the whole wide world has changed with this virus, Corona.

Every single day since the twenty-third of March 2019, has been like a Sunday and all of a sudden you forget what day it really is. It's like time has stood still, like one of those dystopian films, where everyone and everything acts as though there's been some kind of apocalypse, survivors hiding away, streets deserted, a depressive atmosphere all around. I know that sounds over dramatic but all I see is everyone being distanced from each other, all the shops shut except the supermarkets of course where, like locusts, the hoards descended and cleared out all the shelves as if there was going to be a nuclear strike or something and they had to stock up their bunkers – fecking sausages the lot of them! Every day's a Sunday ... Sunday followed by another Sunday ... it's like life was on constant rewind. Groundhog Sunday!

I found myself just praying for the weekend to end so I could do some work. I never thought I would find myself saying that!

I was looking forward to making the second series of *Dan and Paddy's Bucket List* which was in the planning stage, but now we will have to wait until this is all over or until some normality returns before we can return to Japan to film it. How I miss working, it's good for your mind, good for your brain, and good for your soul.

Not being able to go to my church was very difficult for me, I missed church and I never thought I would catch myself thinking thoughts like that but it's a part of my life I need now.

I live in North Wales on a site with other Travellers and no one mixes with anyone, everyone is totally afraid, honest to God, so very afraid for their lives.

274

This has really made me think, thank God me and my brothers, Martin and Dudlow, are able to see each other some of the time, albeit mostly from a distance, over the fence as it were, as we are living on the same site, but I do miss my brothers in London – Kieran, Johnny, Barney, Simey and Tony. I can't wait for it all to end so I can see them again.

We are so very tight knit in the Traveller community and family is everything to us like most people, I guess. I kept dreaming of the end of the lockdown when the pubs would re-open, and I could go and meet my kin for a real good social and a pint.

Of course, my sisters are on the list of people I miss most too – Angela, Mary, Kate, Julie, Margaret and Lizzy. I found myself dreaming about them all, us all having a good craic together one day soon. There's no greater thing in life than the love of your family and when I experienced this lockdown, I missed them so much, like most people, I guess. When we get together for a big social, we all sing! I can't sing to save my life but after a couple of pints I'll give it a go. Some of my brothers tell me I sound like a screeching, wailing banshee, so they cover their ears and pull really pained faces (I can't think why) while I am enjoying every minute of it.

One of the hardest things for me is not being able to go and see my family's graves, pay my respects to my father and my Old Queen along with my brothers Charlie, Tom, Francie and little baby brother Simey, who died at childbirth. Not being able to visit my family's graves was painful for me.

The gates to the cemeteries were locked and although I understand why, it hurt so much not to be able to visit my father and chat with him at his graveside. It was like the world had just pressed the pause button; no planes, busses, everything disappeared, like the world had just stopped dead.

It's just part of my culture, to pay our kin that have passed on, respect and talk to them at certain times. Like my son Patrick whose nickname was 'Spinks'. It hurt so much not to be able to visit him and chat to him.

Roseanne and I are great together most of the time and we get on so well, but I found the lockdown was beginning to wear us both down, being forced together all of the time. Stuck in the same small home can get a little uncomfortable after a while, well more than uncomfortable! So, I found myself going for long walks and cycle rides, often around in circles observing the lockdown instructions, just to give each other some space.

Sometimes when I was so stressed out, and the lockdown rules would allow it, I would jump into my car, go driving, not sure where, no destination in mind, just the open road before me. I would often find myself in the middle of the mountains, in the middle of nowhere, just driving along on my own. The Welsh countryside is so very beautiful, and it would instill such peace in me that when I came back home, I was in fine fettle once more. I love to be able to travel, it's in the blood I guess, and I rediscovered my need to be free and to travel during the lockdown.

Lockdown had given me, like others, plenty of time to think, sometimes perhaps too much time, but I look at life very differently now because of it. Life is completely different from before. It's actually made me think about life. I think we all forget to take stock, to respect life and appreciate life while you have it. We all forget to do that from time to time, to appreciate the ones we love, our woman, our children and grandchildren, they are so very precious, life itself!

Just look at how many lives have been taken by this insidious virus, hundreds and thousands of lives and there seems no end to it… just horrible.

I was so very sorry to hear of the death of a very dear friend of mine, an old man called Christie Joyce – one of the 'Oxford Joyces'. I just could not believe it when I heard the news. His daughters and sons had kept him behind a wall of protection, like a two year old child, wrapped up in cotton wool, and yet the Corona still got him. Tragic for him and so many others. He was still given a great funeral, but it would have been so very much bigger without the restrictions and regulations in force.

What a man he was to me, what a lovely man he was, his wife Winnie was so good too, resting together now. I loved all his family; his sons, sisters and daughters – Joe, Chris, Paddy, Timmy, Mike, Winnie, Margaret and Mary, just great people to me they were and still are. They really were the loveliest people in the world to me and I find immense pleasure to be able to say that about people who are not related to me. It could be said of my dear friend Christie Joyce, that he was like a father figure to me, a strong, good man. I always found it a great honour just to go up to him and shake his hand or give him a kiss. His wife, Winne was a pure lady and the loveliest woman in the world, there really was no nicer woman than her, she was a proper lady. Winnie and Christie were well matched, they were tailor made for each other, like one being the hand and the other the glove, fitting each other so perfectly and snuggly.

Whenever I met the two of them, Winnie and Christie, I would go over and give them both a big hug and a kiss, a real honour to me. God rest the 'Oxford Joyces' as they were known, the loveliest Joyces on the planet, the loveliest Joyces I have and will ever know, and I have known them since I was a small child.

What's sad of course, is the number of people they all leave behind and the list just keeps building the older you get, life is a funny old thing if you are still here. So, in many ways, like a lot of us I suppose, I will be glad to see this year out.

This Corona Virus has made me think about so much and I have decided that really life has been very good to me. I thought life was very bad to me at first and that I was all messed up but in truth, I don't think I really was. I'm realising now perhaps, it's really not been that bad. Then I went and bloody got it didn't I?

It was January, freezing cold, snow flurries all around and I was doing a bit of work on the site, you know, just cleaning up the site, but I wasn't cold. I know when you're doing stuff it can keep you warm, but I was more than warm, I was burning up! Felt like I had a furnace inside me, I could have stripped down into a vest and shorts and still not felt the cold at all!

To cut a long story short, I said to Roseanne, "I've got to lay down, I don't feel good."
I went in, got straight into bed and fell asleep. Knocked out I was. It felt like I hadn't been asleep very long and the next minute Roseanne comes into the house and I'm knocked out, asleep and the bed is drowned, it was drowning in sweat!

She said, "Paddy, I've got to get the ambulance for you…"

"Go away, I'm all right!" I said, "Just change the bed."

So, she changed the bed.

I said, "I'm all right, don't get no ambulance now, I'm OK."

I thought it was just a high temperature but within about half an hour, the bed was drowned again. You'd think I'd wet the bed, or someone had thrown a bucket of water over me, you know? Roseanne starts crying, saying, "Please Paddy? Let me get the ambulance for you?"

I said, "Don't get no one, there's nothing the matter with me."

So, what she done then, was very clever of her! It's about twelve o'clock at night, she's roaring, crying and she phoned up my Margaret; my daughter Margaret has the full balance of me; Margaret's my whole life. She's crying down the phone to our Margaret, "Margaret, Margaret, your Daddy is, your Daddy is on fire, the bed has been drowned a couple of times and he won't let me phone the ambulance!"

She then says, "Paddy, Margaret wants you."

I said, "I don't want to speak to Margaret." Normally I'd never say anything like that about our Margaret, about my child.

I said, "I'm not able to speak to Margaret, Roseanne, just let me close my eyes."

But I couldn't say it all it one go, it took me ages to say it, because my breathing was so bad, I was really struggling to get my breath. So, Margaret's on the phone, I could hear her shouting, "Daddy, Daddy, I am coming down all the way from Scotland. I am coming down now."

This was in January, the snow was really coming down fast, very heavy, it's two hundred and sixty miles to here from where Margaret lives near Aberdeen and I said to my Margaret, "Please, my Margaret, don't be coming down now on that motorway, I'll die if something happens to you, please don't be coming down now."
She's having none of it though, she says, "Daddy, if you don't let Mammy get the ambulance, I'm coming down now!"

You see, I've been funny like this, all my life, I fight things like this, I don't accept that I am sick, I never get sick, I'm never sick! I really believed there was nothing wrong with me because you know, when you feel a bit of the flu coming on, you (well I) just carry on… But the truth is, this time, it just came on really quick, like in a blink! There and then! I really thought I was dying, I was struggling to breathe, I thought I might just go to sleep for a long, long time and never wake up. As usual though I was thinking, 'I'm not letting this kill me, I won't let this kill me.'

I couldn't fight Margaret and Roseanne any longer, even though I thought it was just a temperature or the start of a bit of the flu I had, I didn't think anything was wrong with me but just being able to talk was hard, I was gasping for air, it was taking me ages to just get a few words of protest out and I knew Margaret and Roseanne could hear me wheezing. The thought of my Margaret driving down in those conditions just made me afraid for her, so I gave in and said to Roseanne, "All right woman, do it then, call the ambulance then, call the ambulance."

So, the ambulance arrived and the guys come in, dressed up, in all the special suits, protective gear and I'm thinking 'they look like a pair of sausages!' It looked like a circus… masks, overalls, gloves… like in a film… a *Carry On…* film!
I said to one of them, "I'm OK doctor, honest."
He said, "I'm not a doctor, I'm a paramedic."

"I'm sorry, doctor." I said.

He was like, "Nah, don't worry about it, but I've got a bit of news for you, Paddy."

I said, "Oh, what's that?"

I'm thinking 'Oh, he knows my name!' "You know my name?" I asked him.

"Yeah, I know you, Paddy," he said, "You've got the Corona Virus. COVID-19!"

I said "What? For Fucks Sake! You're kidding me, aren't you?"

"No, not at all, Paddy, you've got it," he said, "without testing, you've got it, I've seen enough of these cases to know that you've got it and you've got it bad," he said again.

"Whoa, Paddy, we've got to get you gone, we've got to get you into that hospital now!" he said.


There was no point in thinking that I wasn't going to go into hospital when the ambulance got here, because of my daughter! You see, Roseanne had her on the phone again and I could hear her saying, "Daddy, I swear, I'm coming down the motorway if you don't get on the ambulance with the men, I'm coming down there!"

I said, "OK, OK, I'm going in the ambulance!"

I couldn't bear the thought of Margaret travelling in that weather, and I knew she would come down. She is married, has a family, she's still my baby and I was worried about her. So, I said to Roseanne, "Roseanne, tell her I'm getting in the ambulance."

Roseanne said, "Margaret, he's getting in the ambulance."

They wouldn't let Roseanne come with me to the hospital and it broke my heart. My Roseanne comes everywhere like that with me, I love her, she is my life and this was the first time she wouldn't be with me. We have a connection beyond belief. I'm no good without her, that's the truth and she's no good without me. I'm a bastard though, I know what I am, listen to this…

I said to her, "Roseanne, give me a kiss."

She said, "What?"

I said, "Give me a kiss, I need a kiss outa my baby."

She kissed me, I said, "OK, if I die, you gotta die, I just passed the Corona to you!" Trying to laugh, coughing and spluttering all over the place, and I could see the paramedic just shaking his head at me in disbelief (but probably laughing on the inside).

"You saying now I'll get the virus, you old bugger?"

We laughed about it though and I told her I'd always visit her grave!

In the ambulance, they put an oxygen mask on me because I couldn't breathe. I could tell it was helping, because my lungs felt like they were starting to open up a bit. The paramedic said to me, "Don't worry, Paddy."
I said, "I'm not worried."

For some reason or another, I knew God would mind me, be behind me, be with me. I've never been afraid to die, I know it's a terrible thing to say, but I'm really not afraid to die. I'm afraid of where I'm going to go, Heaven or Hell, because that's the way I am, I'm afraid that in my life I've done bad things when I was young and everything comes back to bite you sooner or later! I was thinking about some of that stuff. Not violence or robbing or… well some was robbing… I used to rob houses when I was young, but I believe that because of what I did, God made me learn, I mean really, really learn, that what I did was bad and God took my son Patrick to punish me. As true as my father has gone to God, I really thought God had done that to me as punishment, taking one I really loved in the whole wide world, my Patrick, and I never robbed again since then. I'm still not over Patrick now, and my Roseanne will never get over Patrick either.

So, I'm in the ambulance now and it's so funny because they looked like they were going to do some power washing, ridiculous as it sounds, I'm here, thinking 'I'm dying! I'm dying!' and they just look like they are about to do some power washing! We got to the hospital, blue lighted and sirens going full blast all the way!

When the ambulance doors opened, I was at Chester hospital, they ran in with me, wheels spinning, all the lights overhead flashing by making my eyes hurt and they dropped me at the area reserved for COVID patients. Immediately I was surrounded by five or six people all in the head-to-toe protective suits, doctors and nurses. They took all my clothes off me, no, they cut them off me and dumped them in a contaminations bin. They put me in a gown and a fastened a wristband tag onto me and said, "Mr Doherty, you are seriously, seriously poorly." They put another oxygen mask on me, it looked like a scuba diving mask and said again, "Mr Doherty, you are seriously poorly." I didn't know which one was talking to me but I knew at that point they were telling me I was dying.

I was so tired and weak I just said, "All right then, please, I just need to go to sleep,"

"No, you can't sleep Mr Doherty."

I said, "Call me Paddy, please call me Paddy."

"Paddy, you can't sleep, you cannot go to sleep yet…" and they kept me awake doing tests, taking blood, hooking me up to electronic stuff. I felt like I was some kind of bloody experiment gone wrong. I was in and out of awareness, I just wanted to sleep, but every time I closed my eyes, someone else was at me, prodding and poking, keeping me from the blissful sleep I wanted.

I couldn't believe it, within twenty minutes, I was up on this COVID-19 ward. It smelled funny, like a mix of bleach, disinfectant and death, you know that sort of underlying, cloying sickly smell. Aren't you supposed to lose your sense of smell and taste when you get COVID? At that point, I would have liked nothing more!

There were five other men on that ward with me. The lighting was dim, the beds all lined up in a row, hooked into the walls by loads of wires, no visitors' chairs, no bedside cabinets for personal belongings, no tray on wheels, now flowers or cards, just super clinical with big yellow bins all over the place and 'Martians' milling about the beds. All you could hear was the rattling of their breathing, them trying to breathe, the beeping of the machines and it felt so lonely. No one was allowed to visit; I didn't know anyone else there. I knew I was on a ward where one day you were here and gone the next. I actually saw them wheeling dead people out and new patients in, like a conveyor belt on the *Generation Game*, but you don't get prizes, just death!

I said to the man in the next bed to me, "Have you been here long?"

"No, I've not," he said, "I'll be dead tomorrow."

I said, "Don't say that my old uncle, don't say that, leave it to God, you'll be all right, it'll be all right." I said.

He didn't die, well I don't think he died anyhow, but it was very sad.

While I was in there, three of the six of us died and were wheeled away to God knows where.

We were all wearing the scuba diving style masks, you know, like the one the Prime Minister was wearing. These are the ones they put you on just before you have to go on to a ventilator.

The doctor came on his rounds and he said to me, "Are you all right Paddy?"

I said, "I am doctor, thank you. How do you know my name?" I asked.

He said, "Oh, I know all about you, Paddy!" He'd obviously done a bit of research on me or something, because he spun one on me, he worked me and he got me good! Being all nice and friendly like. He even went so far as to tell me not to call him doctor, but to call him Frank (I can't remember the actual name now, so I'll just use Frank for now). Anyhow, we were chatting for about twenty minutes, but he was doing most of the chatting, because I couldn't talk much for my breathing. He was asking me what I knew about steroids and whether I'd ever used any in the past. I told him that I knew you could get bad ones and good ones. I told him I used to take steroids when I was a young lad but not for years and years now. I was getting a bit suspicious with the line of questioning…

He asked, "What do you do if you get a bad steroid?"

I said, "I pay the man who gave them to me."

"Why would you do that?" he asked.

I said, "Because, I'm taking his word that they have to be good steroids needed for the weightlifting and stuff. Then if they weren't good, I'd really PAY the man, if you know what I mean? That was the world I was in then, that's the life I lived."

So, then he said, "Well, I'm going to give you a steroid," this is where he got me lovely!

I said "Yeah?"

He said, "Are you not frightened, don't you think you should ask me what kind of steroids they are?"

I said, "Doctor…"

"No! there you go again, don't call me doctor… Frank," he said.

I said, "I'm sorry, Frank. Well, it's the NHS, they have to be good steroids. I'm getting them off the NHS, so I know anything you're going to put inside of me is good!"

"Well Paddy, I'd like to show you these steroids."

I am not kidding you, he brought out these two bottles, about the same size as the small bottles of water you can get from the shop. They had two needles as big as a writing pen on top of them!

I said, "You're not putting them inside of me! Come on! They are not going inside of me!"

Then he said, "Do you not think you should ask me what they are?"

"I don't care what they are! Doctor or not, they're not going inside of me!" I said.

He said, "I think you should ask me what they are and my name is not doctor, it's FRANK!"

I said, "I'm sorry, Frank, but you're not putting them jokes inside of me!"

He said, "You took steroids for years," he held them up to me and said, "You call these 'YOU LIVE'," then he put them down on the bed and held up his empty hands and said, "and you call this 'YOU DIE', what's it gonna be, Paddy?"

I knew what he meant straight away, but to be sure, I asked, "Frank, what did you say? What are you meaning?"

He said, "You take it, you live, you don't take it, you die Paddy!"

Now, I never knew a doctor could tell you this, but they had to be blunt with everything. "That's it then Paddy."

I said, "Well then, I'm fucked, I'm fucked either way!"

Two doctors came up beside me and I said, "Go on then, I'll take it."

So, I had one doctor on each side of me and one of them said, "Paddy, what's that over there?"

I turned in the direction he was looking and said, "Where…?" As I said that and I'm looking 'over there,' the bugger stuck me in my belly! I was squirming and it felt like they were at me with these massive needles for an hour, but I knew really it wasn't, it was just a couple of minutes and I was knocked clean out then.

I lost a whole day then and didn't realise it. Not long after I woke up Frank came round and he goes, "You all right, Paddy?"

"I am, Frank."

"Oh, you remember me? Well, I've got fantastic news to tell you." he said.

"What's that?" I asked.

"You're going to live!" he said. "Paddy, we can't make people take our medicine. We cannot. It's against the law. You're a Traveller and you don't know much about that. I did a lot of research on you, and I knew how stubborn, how stick you can be, so I got you and worked you until you relaxed and that's when I jabbed you. But know this, if you hadn't taken it then, you would be dead now."

You're on your own. I couldn't even talk to those around me, the ones that survived and those that didn't before they died. Like me, they weren't able to talk much, their breathing was so bad, hardly any breath for talking. Those that did said to me, "You're full of life, Paddy Doherty!" So, I tried my best to cheer them up, I was always pulling their legs, having a laugh, trying to make their situation better, bearable, you know?

I was struggling though; I wouldn't let nobody see my body broke down when I was badly smashed up. This was worse than any pain I had before, I've had a couple of bad beatings, but they don't compare to this. My body dropped down so much in weight and I've never experienced that before. I'm still not good out of it either, I can't believe that my body is still broke down from it now. The doctor said to me, "It's going to take nine months, Paddy. You had a serious bout, you were severely affected by it, it's going to take nine months for your lungs to clear from such a serious bout, for your lungs to fully recover."

I was in hospital for eight days in total and at this point I
knew I was going to live, even though I'm not afraid to die,
I'm afraid of where I'm going to go, I'm afraid of my life for
that, but I'm not afraid to die. I was going to live. All I could
think about was my Roseanne, my Margaret, my sons, I was
so lonely, all alone, because I was on my own, no one allowed
to visit, people dying all around me, no one there to hold
their hands or anything like that, that's COVID for you. So
sad, it's unbelievable.

I was doing a bike ride, as I was advised, you know when you
get advised, don't be that thick that you don't listen. But I felt
so old, you don't realise, you think you're still young and fit,
but you're not. You think no one can beat youth, youth is
everything, my body's aching all the time now. One man told
me that when you get COVID, it takes two years to fully
recover, get back to what you were before. I'm still on
treatment at this time, I get so tired, I'm always falling asleep,
even when I'm driving, I have to pull in to sleep! My body
just tells me it needs it! A lot of people used to come to my
mother's, I used to say, "I'm just going upstairs for ten

minutes." My eyes would close and whether it's ten minutes or an hour later, life was back in me for a little while.

I wouldn't wish COVID-19 on my worst enemy (if I had any!). My experience with it is probably no different than anyone else's, except maybe in severity. Don't be a stubborn mule! Know when you need to ask for help; when you know you need to go into hospital. Go. Get the help you need. Those NHS staff are so awesome, putting themselves in danger like that every single day. Yes, the needles are scary! But like the doc said, "with it you live, without it, you die!"

I'm so glad I am still here, still recovering, but at least I am alive! It could have turned out very differently!

## _My God_

Some people are religious, some people aren't or don't actively practice their faith. That is entirely up to them. People also have opinions about other peoples' belief systems, which is okay, because after all, everyone is entitled to an opinion, whether you or me agree with it or not. Like many Travellers, I was raised to believe in the Christian faith, so what follows are my own thoughts and experiences only. Of course, if you are not religious then I respect your choice and your opinion. Like I said, it's not for everyone, it's a personal thing, I get that.

Remember, God doesn't look for you, God doesn't go looking for anyone, you've got to go and look for God yourself. When you find God in your life, it's the greatest gift in the world. Since I found God, I have got so much more peace, personally, I am so glad that I found God.

Although I say I'm a Christian, I am certainly not the greatest Christian. I drink. I used to drink an awful lot and be a bit messed up with my nerves. Thank God I don't drink much at all now, maybe once a week or on the odd occasion if something comes up when I might drink two days in a row but no more than that.

As Gloria Gaynor sang: '*I am what I am….*' And that goes for me too!

As it says in the *Bible*, you have to forgive and if you don't forgive you cannot enter the Kingdom of Heaven.

I would love to go to Heaven when I die. I don't know if I will but I hope I do. I have tried to forgive though and apologise for my sins. I am so glad that I found God again.

Dan Rooney was a legend who fought anyone, he was simply the best. He had such a great name and was never beaten, bred for fighting and now, believe it or not, he has become a pastor, and works with God every day.

People now though, try to slag him off when he goes around preaching just because he used to be a fighter and now they see him as a fool, even the women look doubtful, thinking it's just some act, but I'm telling you, you can't be fooled or a fool when you are talking to God or a man of God. This man is just like a disciple of God to me.

This man is one of my heroes amongst all the Travellers of

the world, this man is something else. Genuinely, he is my hero. The only thing he is not, which I would absolutely love, is he's not my brother. He is one of the reasons I got into religion. I was always a Catholic, not a practising one, but what this man did, just turning his back on the fighting, not caring what people were saying or thinking about him. His approach was to let this be whatever it was, didn't bother him, he just changed his life completely. He is a plain and simply fantastic man of God. He had a name like a racehorse. People now slag him of course, saying, 'look at that fool, who does he think he is?' Well to me, when you talk of God and become the sort of man he has become, you can't be beaten still. He is a great man of God.

My wife gave herself to God years ago and knew all about pastors, so she introduced me to Billy Winters. He didn't go straight in with the full-on preaching thing, but instead he reeled me in slowly and when my sister Margaret was dying, he was always there in the background, asking how she was. "Don't worry Patrick, God will look after her," he would say to me.
He was always talking about God and His works to me and he encouraged me to come down to his church. He said I

could just come along and stay for as long or as little as I liked – I'd be free to walk out at any time.  One day I gave it a go. I went for a short time at first, then a bit longer and then a bit longer still and before I knew it I was going regularly and staying for the full service. I always wanted to hear Billy Winters speak. He made a connection, it felt like he was just talking to me directly. It changed me for the better and now, thanks to him, I have God in my heart. He is a great man; he has a lovely wife and his son is a real young gentleman. I thank Billy Winters for helping me become a Christian again and I feel that God sent him to me. It doesn't suit everyone but it suits me.

I have forgiven all of my enemies, if I had them, because if you don't know how to forgive people it can affect who you become, it's like an internal sadness and you just carry bitterness and sadness with you. As it says in the *Bible*: '*If you don't know how to forgive and forgive people, then you can't enter the Kingdom of Heaven.*' For me Heaven is the greatest reward. There is no way of describing what it is like, but I imagine it's something completely out of this world and then go a hundred million times better than that – to me that is what Heaven would be like.

If you don't forgive, I believe you carry bitterness, sadness and shame around with you all the time. It eats into you and affects the way you are with people and how they see you too. If you have an argument with a daughter or a son for example, you have to forgive.

I still get angry at things, but even with my anger I have found that time is a great healer and now I find I have so much peace in my heart. I don't hang on to bitterness, hatred and vengeance anymore.

When I swear now, I feel so guilty, or if I tell a lie, I say to myself, 'I SHOULD NOT BE SAYING THAT!' I may see something and think, in all honesty, 'I could take that, I could rob that!' Now that's being truthful, we all could do that. We might see something, we could be off with it, and no one would know that we had done it. Well, I just would not do it. I truly would not take a thing that was not mine and I can't say in all honesty, that it would not have been the case years ago. So now, I will not steal anything.

I love life and I pray every day for my wife to get stronger and be okay. I pray for God to help me and make me a better person and to make me strong and watch over my children. I pray for my mother to be strong and my brothers and sisters on both sides and all my family to be strong and happy too. I particularly pray a great deal for my sister who has had depression since losing her son Michael.

Poor Micky Connors had so very much to live for, a well to do man, great looking, big stud farm, lovely family, great business, he had everything going for him. Then he died in a terrible accident but God wanted him, so he took him. When God wants you, he will take you it seems to me, no matter who you are or what you are.

I need God in my life and I certainly love life more because of it. God sees and hears everything but no one sees God watching in that way.

If it is God's will that I die tomorrow, then I really don't care. That may sound a little selfish, but it's not sad for me. I have just reached a point in my life where I really don't feel as if I care too much if I live or die. I have felt this for a few years now. I can hear my voice saying to me in my head, 'You're very selfish, Paddy,' but I don't feel selfish, and to my mind I am far from selfish.

But from the bottom of my heart, truth, I really don't care when I die. I remember when I had the trouble with my prostate and I realised at that point that I really was not at all afraid of death. My father was afraid of dying, God rest his soul. I never knew my father could be afraid of anything until I saw him being afraid of death.

What I am afraid of is going to Hell, I live in fear of that all right! I am not afraid of death because I know I have a chance of not going to Hell and making it into Heaven. But if I don't then I am in the fires of Hell for the whole of eternity. That is my greatest fear!

I don't fear death itself. Some of you might say: 'Paddy Doherty – you are a sick mental patient,' but I don't see it like that. I remember seeing the fear in my father's eyes like I have never seen before in my life, and I have to say that it woke me up sharp. That sight woke me up to the realisation that I should get myself right with God. I don't feel I'm absolutely right with Him yet, but I am trying my best and God, no doubt, helps me move this way and that. I am getting better at it all with time.

During the COVID-19 lockdown and while I was in hospital, not being able to go to my church was very difficult for me, I missed church and I never thought I would catch myself thinking thoughts like that but it's a part of my life I need now.

While I was driving the car one day, I pressed a button on the radio looking for something good to listen to and by chance, I came across a station that was playing Christians reading bits from the *Bible* and telling stories from the gospels and singing lovely Christian songs. Well this really made my day, so much so, that I won't let anyone touch the radio controls now because I am afraid to lose the channel and I might not be able to get it back!

While my heart is with God, it keeps me on the straight and narrow and I don't do half the things I used to do, the wrong things. I know it's not for everyone but it works for me. I now find it *'easy to love my neighbour as I do myself'*. Love my brothers and sisters as I do myself. At one time in my life I had lots of enemies and I can honestly say I do not have enemies anymore.

At the end of the day, God is going to be my judge, so I am not afraid. I swear on my son's grave I am not afraid.

I do believe that God performs miracles every second of every day of the week, we just don't see it. I feel my God performed a miracle on me when I was shot in the head, had the prostate cancer and then the Corona Virus. I truly believe He left me here for a reason and to do something good with my time left. I hope I don't let Him down.

Heaven is a great gift and the biggest of all gifts is to have God in my life, I certainly need Him. I hope I am explaining this right? It's not for everyone but it is for me and I love life more because of it.

## _Mortality_

To die or not to die – that is the question.

I don't want to die right now, of course, but if I did then what choice have I but to accept it? I am not afraid to die. A bit of me is looking forward to dying, I would love to die. I know that is really sad, and perhaps some people will think me a little selfish or crazy for saying it. These feelings come and go in me though and I don't really understand why.

I know there are people fighting for their lives in hospitals and at home, fighting all sorts of things like cancer and other terminal illnesses and there are those living in countries where their lives are at risk every day, begging, hoping and praying, just for a few more years of life and yet I feel I have got to a stage now where I would not miss anything in this life, if I were to die.

Some people are afraid to die, but I am not afraid, even today. I can put my hand on my heart and say I am not afraid to die. I don't mean that in a bad way, I mean that in a good way. If I die tomorrow morning, if I die today or the doctor tells me my time is up, well that's that and I will accept it.

We have this Corona going around at the moment, but I have to say and on my life this is the truth, I know people are fighting for their lives, and it is a shameful thing, but I believe that if it is God's will and I die tomorrow or next week or six weeks' time, or six months, I really don't care if I live or die.

Now I know that is sad and may sound a little selfish to be honest. Well, it's not sad for me actually, I have just got to the point in my life where I really don't feel as if I care too much if I live or die.

I have had this feeling in my head for a lot of years now. My voice says to me in my head, 'Your very selfish Paddy,' I am not selfish, I am far from selfish as I would think anyhow.

My Roseanne, I adore her but I am not always sure she adores me, we are drifting, no one knows that. It's funny how I find myself to be able to talk about this here when I have not said this to anyone I know. Maybe, deep down, this is what is behind my thoughts and acceptance of death, if it decided to take me? I know it would hurt a lot of people but by the way I feel just now, I swear on my son Patrick's grave, if I died this minute, if I died this week, next month, two month, six months or five years from now. God forgive me for saying this it would never bother me. If someone said to me Paddy Doherty you've got fourteen days left on this planet, I would say, "Thank you!" And I mean that. I am talking now from my heart.

I think, 'Who would really miss you?' Nobody really but your own family members. Everyone misses you for a while, but everyone has to move on and get on with life when you are gone. Everyone moves on; it's life; it's only natural. You have to make as much of life as you can - it's the Traveller way.

I would give all my organs to anyone who needs them, any part of my physical body can go to help anyone if it is needed, apart from my brain because I have a bad, mixed up brain, I have bad thoughts and good thoughts constantly coming into my head and cannot switch them off, with far too many bad thoughts continually cooking away in my head.

So let my brain rot away but let my heart, eyes, kidneys, liver, lungs any part of my body let it be used if it can, to improve someone's life after my death.

At the end of the day, God is going to be my judge, so I am not afraid. I swear on my son's grave; I am not afraid.

I am sure you will all agree with me, when you look around at your brothers, sisters, family members and close friends who you have grown up with, we might look old as we get to a certain point in our lives but we all still feel young!

Of course, in our minds and hearts we still feel like we're young, like we were in our thirties and forties and long may that continue, but at the same time, we only have to look in the mirror to see we are moving on in age or our bodies let us know that is the case too, don't they? You just have to find a way to live with that. You know, it's a bit like your name, Doherty, Rooney, Cash or McQueen or whatever it may be; your name lives on in the impressions you make on people, the positive impacts you have on their lives and most of all, it lives on in your children and your children's children.

Remember to live life to the fullest, find the happiness inside you, make a difference if you can, the past can't be changed, everyone's journey is different, smiles are contagious and kindness is free.

Printed in Great Britain
by Amazon